For Jayne,
with gratitude & love,

Mary Foster Hutchinson

HOLY HERITAGE

AN INFORMAL HISTORY OF THE
CATHEDRAL CHURCH OF ST. MATTHEW
IN DALLAS, TEXAS,
ITS ANCESTRY,
AND THE CITY IT SERVES

BY

MARY FOSTER HUTCHINSON

WITH A LOOK FORWARD
BY THE VERY REVEREND NEAL OTIS MICHELL, D.MIN.
DEAN OF SAINT MATTHEW'S CATHEDRAL

Copyright © 2016 Mary Foster Hutchinson.

All rights reserved. No part of this book may be used or reproduced by any means, graphic, electronic, or mechanical, including photocopying, recording, taping or by any information storage retrieval system without the written permission of the author except in the case of brief quotations embodied in critical articles and reviews.

WestBow Press books may be ordered through booksellers or by contacting:

WestBow Press
A Division of Thomas Nelson & Zondervan
1663 Liberty Drive
Bloomington, IN 47403
www.westbowpress.com
1 (866) 928-1240

Because of the dynamic nature of the Internet, any web addresses or links contained in this book may have changed since publication and may no longer be valid. The views expressed in this work are solely those of the author and do not necessarily reflect the views of the publisher, and the publisher hereby disclaims any responsibility for them.

Any people depicted in stock imagery provided by Thinkstock are models, and such images are being used for illustrative purposes only. Certain stock imagery © Thinkstock.

ISBN: 978-1-5127-2001-3 (sc)
ISBN: 978-1-5127-2003-7 (hc)
ISBN: 978-1-5127-2002-0 (e)

Library of Congress Control Number: 2015918874

Print information available on the last page.

WestBow Press rev. date: 4/8/2016

THIS IS NONE OTHER BUT THE HOUSE OF GOD; THIS IS THE GATE OF HEAVEN

Genesis 29:17

IN GRATITUDE FOR THE LOVING SERVICE OF

THE RIGHT REVEREND JAMES MONTE STANTON

SIXTH BISHOP OF DALLAS

PRO POPULO DEI

SAINT MATTHEW WRITING HIS EPISTLE
The Lindisfarne Gospel
AD 700

CONTENTS

I. THE BOOK OF EVANGELISTS

Chapter One - The Explorers...1
- The First Dallasites 1
- Texas Enters Written History 2
- The Spanish Mission, Part 1..4
- The Spanish Mission Part 2...6
- The First Empresario..7
- The Anglican Mission - Part 1..10

Chapter Two - The Settlers 15
- A Feeble New Country...15
- A Cultural Revolution..17
- The Last Empresarios...19
- The Mercer Colony 20
- The Birth of a Village 21
- A Failed Paradise: The Rise and Fall of La Reunion......25

Chapter Three - The Founders 29
- The Anglican Mission Part 2 29
- George Rottenstein..29
- Why Saint Matthew?...33
- A Birthday into Heaven 35

II. THE BOOK OF MINISTERS

Chapter Four - A Dignity of Bishops 41
    A Firm Foundation 43
    Leonidas Polk, the Fighting Bishop 43
    George Washington Freeman, the Provisional Bishop 44
    James Alexander Gregg, the Dixie Bishop 45
    Alexander Charles Garrett, the Bishop -
        Presiding Bishop 47
    "Ride Like Cowboys, Pray Like Saints" 49
    Harry Tunis Moore, Dean, Coadjutor, and Bishop 51
    Charles Avery Mason, - the Cornerstone Bishop 52
    Archibald Donald Davies - the Schismatic Bishop 54
    Donis Dean Patterson, the Transitional Bishop 56
    James Monte Stanton - the Theological Bishop 57

Chapter Five - Our First Very Reverends 61
    Silas Deane Davenport - 2nd Rector, 1st Dean 64
    Stephen Herbert Green, the High Church Dean 68
    A Second Cathedral 68
    John Davis, the Erudite Dean 70
    William Munford, the Soldier Dean 72
    Charles William Turner, the English Dean 73
    The Third Cathedral 74
    James Hudson Stuck, the Alaskan Dean 76
    The Call of the Wild 79

Chapter Six - A Transforming Half-Century 81
    George Edward Walk, the Linguist Dean 82
    Harry Tunis Moore. Dean and Bishop 83
    Jackson H. R. Ray, the Mad Dean of Dallas 84
    Robert Scott Chalmers, the Scottish Dean 87
    George Rodgers Wood, the Disquieted Dean 92
    Murder of a Cathedral 92

    Gerald Grattan Moore, the Gentle Dean 94
    Frank Locke Carruthers, a Transitional Dean 98

Chapter Seven - Stained Glass 101
    Charles Preston Wiles, the Naval Dean.......................... 102
    Ernest Edward Hunt III, the International Dean.......... 106
    Philip Menzie Duncan II, the Floridian Dean 107
    Michael Shane Mills, the Alabaman Dean 109
    Kevin Eugene Martin, the Valiant Dean........................ 111
    Neal Otis Michell, the First Native Born Texan and
        Current Dean 113

Looking Forward.. 115

Chronology... 121

Works Consulted 125

Acknowledgements 129

TRANSIENS ADIUVANOS
(WE CROSS THE SEAS TO GIVE HELP)
Motto of the Church of England Missionary Society

I. THE BOOK OF EVANGELISTS

THIS IS THE STORY OF THE CATHEDRAL CHURCH OF SAINT MATTHEW,

IN THE EPISCOPAL DIOCESE OF DALLAS

BUT WAIT !

A CHURCH,

ESPECIALLY A CATHEDRAL CHURCH,

DOESN'T JUST RISE SPONTANEOUSLY

OUT OF PRIMORDIAL MUD!

Before there was a CATHEDRAL there had to be a PARISH!

And before there was a PARISH there had to be a VILLAGE!

And before there was a VILLAGE there had to be PIONEERS!

And before there were PIONEERS there had to be LAND!

THAT IS WHERE THIS TALE BEGINS -

IN A LAND CALLED TEXAS!

CHAPTER ONE
THE EXPLORERS

The First Dallasites

Dallas and its surrounds are not very old, only a dot, really, or maybe a blob on the scroll of geographic history. But if its cathedral did not descend full grown from the clouds, neither did what we now call the Metroplex. It has a past. It has one of the most remote prehistorical pasts in America.

Go up to the Aubrey Site on the Elm Fork of the Trinity River below Lake Ray Roberts Dam and visit in your imagination the Stone Age people who lived there ten thousand years ago. True, we know almost nothing about them. They crossed into our continent during the Pleistocene Era on a land bridge from Siberia. They were omnivores, living on herbs, nuts, fruit, and roots, and (when they could get it) the meat of enormous animals - bison twice as large as the modern kind, extinct elephants, and mammoths, - which they killed with spears. (Bows and arrows had not yet been invented.)

Apart from these meager facts, history stumbles, but anthropologists tell us that these folk were physically just like us. They shivered when the blue northers descended and basked in the largess of spring. They were miserable. They were ecstatic. They were just as smart as we are. (Could any of us figure out how to kill a mammoth with a wooden spear and use his carcass to fulfill all our needs - food, clothing, shelter, the works?) They were fully human. They were us. Within them lurked the same spirit which animates all men, which animates us. History and science have concluded that they believed in an after-life. I believe that they had souls.

What feeble creatures they were to carry so great a burden! But then, so are we. Primitive as they were, they must have had, as we do, an innate longing for an undefined infinite. They must have gazed in awe just as we do at the star-studded immensity of space, on their way to Tierra del Fuego, on their way to Bethlehem. Maybe they took a wrong turn. Maybe they were looking on the wrong continent, dreaming that some day Bethlehem would come to them.

It came. But it was a long time coming.

Most histories shy away from pointing out that ancient man had a spiritual side, even that all men have a spiritual side, in the former case because the evidence is thin (although not completely lacking), in the latter case because faith is controversial and controversial has come to mean irrelevant. But this tale of St. Matthew's is a religious tale. From the beginning, we have had a religious history. We have not forgotten you, old people.

Texas Enters Written History

It is human nature to want to know what lies beyond the sunset. Maybe it is better hunting. More bison, maybe. More roots and berries. Maybe fame. Maybe gold. Maybe just the freedom to be alone. It has many names, but they all have the same root. SAINT AUGUSTINE OF HIPPO got it right. *Our hearts are restless until they rest in Thee, O Lord.* Everyone feels it. Not everyone knows what it is. Everyone chases it. Not everyone finds it. In the fifteenth century it beckoned from across the Western Sea.

Texas began modern life in 1493 through what must have been one of the greatest real estate swindles of all time when POPE ALEXANDER VI divided the American discoveries of CHRISTOPHER COLUMBUS between Spain and Portugal.

Holy Heritage

Columbus, of course, was not the first European to chance upon and attempt to colonize North America. The Vikings' and probably the Scots' doomed attempts beat him by several hundred years. But this time, backed by the might of the world's greatest political power, the spiritual strength of the papacy, and a bit of global warming, the discovery lasted. The area which would be known some day as Texas (derived from a Caddo word meaning *friends*) fell to the lot of Spain, which maintained sovereignty for three hundred and twenty-eight years, except for a brief five-year period when RENE ROBERT CAVALIER, SIEUR DE LA SALLE, flew the fleur-de-lys over Matagorda Bay.

The land called Texas was immense, stretching from the Gulf of Mexico (which the Spaniards called the North Sea) up to the Red River, reaching still farther north and west to include half of what is now New Mexico, one third of what is now Colorado, and substantial bites of Kansas, Oklahoma, and Wyoming. At the time of conquest this gorgeous, massive, brutish dominion was inhabited by three principal races: the Pueblo in the upper Rio Grande area, the Mississippian mound builders in the middle, and the Mesoamericans of the south, their dozens of sub-tribes as distinct from one another as France is from Russia today. Believing that he had found a water route to the Asian subcontinent, Columbus called them all Indians. The name stuck.

The Spaniards were not tardy in trying their luck in the vastness they called New Spain. America became not only a source of political power but also a mine of treasure both mineral and human. South of the Rio Grande (which the Spanish knew as the Rio Bravo), fantastic amounts of gold waited to be looted, some of which can still be seen by tourists today while visiting the Chapel Royal in Granada. The bones of thousands of native slaves dusted the splendor of Spanish America south of the Rio Bravo. Franciscan friars did their best to teach the surviving aborigines to settle down and become farmers, then converts, and to accept European-like ways. Many did. North of the Rio Bravo, not so many.

The Spanish Mission, Part 1

Texas was lucky in its first European visitor and first Christian missionary. SENOR ALVAR NUNEZ CABEZA DE VACA, a soldier born into a noble Spanish family, was second in command of an expedition of 300 men sent by the King of Spain in 1527 to explore that part of his new domain called Florida. Two hundred and ninety seven of these stalwarts never saw Spain again. Eight years and 6,000 miles later Mr. Cow-Head (as his name translates) and three companions (one an African), stumbled into Mexico City, naked and starving. Their amazing tale, preserved as Cabeza de Vaca's *Adventures in the Unknown Interior of America*, is not only a geographic and archaeological treasure but also the tale of a spiritual journey.

Like most of his contemporaries, Cabeza de Vaca had sailed to America seeking gold and glory. He ended up pursuing a greater goal. *"To bring all these people to Christianity,"* he wrote, *"they must be won by kindness, the only certain way."* He set a missionary standard for all who came after him.

Cabeza de Vaca spent considerable time on the Isle of Doom (Galveston Island, to us), and traded gourds through what is now known as the Texas Hill Country, moving north almost to Oklahoma, possibly near enough to the site of present-day Dallas (it is hard to tell) to be called the first European to wet his feet in the Trinity River.

Many not-so-spiritual Europeans followed, seeking slaves and treasure. FRANCISCO VASQUEZ DE CORONADO passed through in 1541 chasing the legendary Seven Cities of Cibola. LUIS MOSCESO DE ALVARADO, second in command of the HERNANDO DE SOTO exploration, gave North Texas a cursory glance in 1542. Finding it poor, he withdrew.

In 1689, ALONSO DE LEON, running into our river 200 miles south of its partition, named it the River of the Holy Trinity. Whether he intended a physical description (actually, it has four branches, not three) or a nod at a religious holiday is unknown.

Holy Heritage

The Trinity River never received much attention because it was not usefully navigable, leaving the future site of Dallas isolated and undiscovered. From time to time, romantic figures like Frenchman LOUIS DE ST. DENIS and his pretty Mexican wife passed through the future Dallas. But Texas was not yet ready to adopt any nationality. So far as Dallas was concerned, nothing much came of any of these visitations.

In the eighteenth century, the French owned a vast territory to the east of Texas called Louisiana. In some of the tentative maps they drew, Louisiana seemed to include parts of North Texas. When, in 1762, France turned Louisiana over to Spain, many Frenchmen remained where they were and continued life as Spanish citizens. One of these, a French trader called ATHENESE DE MIEZIERES (son-in-law of aforementioned Louis de St. Denis), camped out during hunting season on a bluff overlooking the Trinity River. (Those who doubt that Dallas has bluffs can drive out Singleton/Hampton Road and stand on one.) Considered an area expert, De Miezieres was appointed Governor of Texas in 1779, the first to be so denominated, but died before he could assume his office. He is principally remembered because sixty-two years later JOHN NEELY BRYAN would choose de Miezieres' camp as the site for his log cabin

While all this was going on, northern Europeans, especially the English, were ignoring the Pope's gifts and establishing themselves in eastern North America. When the United States was born and began to grow, its citizens felt an increasing annoyance that such a large bite of North America as Spain still claimed should stand in the way of their dream of western expansion. In 1800, as Hispanic power waned in Europe, Spain signed Louisiana back over to France. Maps were still imperfect and borders speculative, so much so that in 1803, when the United States purchased Louisiana from France, the USA assumed that Texas was included in her acquisition. Spain contested, on the grounds that Texas had never been part of Louisiana in the first place. A special agreement, the Adam-Onis Treaty, settled the matter in Spain's favor. Texas remained a Spanish colony. U.S. citizens felt cheated. American eyes began to be focused on Texas as the natural next step in their drive toward the Pacific. Texas, they felt, ought to be theirs.

The Spanish Mission Part 2

Spain regarded the New World as a miser regards his strongbox, but it wasn't just a source of wealth. It was also an empire to be conquered and populated, containing savages who needed to be Christianized and civilized. South of the Rio Bravo, much of this was accomplished, but to the north, rather less. It was not that Spain did not try to do something with her northern stepchild, but Texas was a sad disappointment to the Spanish government. Texas had a bad reputation. Few Hispanics wanted to live here. Unlike Mexico and Central America we offered no rich mines and few savages waiting around to be captured and sold as slaves. Thirty Franciscan missions were established in Texas to maintain Spanish sovereignty and teach the Roman faith, but one by one each withered. Texas Indians were different from those in Mexico, harder to convert to European ways. Many were wiped out by imported European diseases. Some died of despair.

Spanish settlers in Texas fared little better. It is arguable that in a classic case of unintended consequences the Hispanic colonizers brought the seeds of their own destruction with them. Sixteenth century Spain was just emerging from five hundred years of occupation by the Moors. When the Spaniards entered Texas, they rode a Moorish animal, heretofore unknown here, called a horse. These hardy Barb and Arab beasts, unlike the steeds of northern Europe, were accustomed to hot, dry climates and were bred for toughness, resilience, and speed. A warlike tribe called the Comanches (a Ute word meaning *always my enemy*) took to these odd animals and became, according to at least one authority, the finest horsemen ever known. Fierce and relentless, they helped to ravage the thirty missions which had been set out so hopefully to convert and civilize. In 1795, Spain's last surviving Texas mission, San Antonio de Valero, was reluctantly secularized and its property dispersed.

In addition to dangerous natives, another barrier separated civilized Mexico from wild Texas. An uninhabited desert (the *desplobada*) lay between the Rio Bravo and the Rio de la Nueces. Few Spaniards cared to cross this barricade. Even convicts promised remission of their sentences refused to colonize Texas. Eventually all attempts at Spanish colonization ceased. Yet a settled and loyal population of some kind was urgently needed both as a deterrent to the Comanche devastation and as a buffer between New Spain and its hereditary enemy, the growing Anglo-Saxon nation called the USA. Reluctantly, New Spain decided to open immigration to non-Spanish Europeans.

The First Empresario

The government of New Spain had an ingenious method for distributing land. It granted enormous tracts to individuals called empresarios in return for a promise to plant thereon a stated number of settlers within a stated number of years. The empresario system had first been tried in Missouri in the early eighteen hundreds when that territory was part of Louisiana. Why not try it in Texas?

Today it seems odd that so many American citizens were eager to emigrate to a foreign province, one with an alien tongue and, for most of Protestant America, an alien religion. It is important to remember, however, that the modern idea of patriotism was not yet fully formed in the mid-nineteenth century. Few U.S. citizens felt the kind of loyalty that has developed in our country after two World Wars. True, the words to the *Star Spangled Banner* had been written during the War of 1812, but this poem was not put to a tavern tune and adopted as national anthem until 1931, one hundred and ten years after the first U.S. citizens immigrated to Texas.

Before then, Americans were aware of no need for a national

anthem and felt little loyalty to Washington D.C., especially in the south. Folk who moved westward planned to take their culture with them. They knew from experience that they had the intelligence and gumption to do this. Public Relations were already at work. They were seduced by the honeyed words of the speculators, wrongly attributing to Texas a mild climate with a healthy carpet of grasslands, well watered, and framed with banks of flowers.

What Texas actually did offer was teeming acres of largely free land. Land ownership mattered. Even in America, the European notion that the possession of land gave social, political and economic standing was strong. Furthermore, coupled with the hope of personal prestige and the need for physical expansion, Texas provided U. S. citizens with an escape hatch from the collapse of their economy, which had bottomed out in the Financial Panic of 1819. Money troubles were everywhere. Indeed, one of Texas' earliest promoters, a man from Missouri named MOSES AUSTIN, languished in debtors' prison. And he wasn't the only impecunious American behind bars.

Moses Austin seemed at the moment to be an unlikely empire builder. But he should occupy the place of honor in any list of Texas' political fathers. Moses had been an early observer of the empresario system when it was originally tried in Missouri. When the political climate seemed favorable, he thought he could use his prior knowledge to repair his fortune in New Spain.

Having served his penal sentence, Moses traveled confidently to Bexar, (headquarters of Governor of Texas, DON ANTONIO MARTINEZ), to file his application to become an Empresario in Texas. He was denied. The Spaniards felt, reasonably enough, that they would lose Texas altogether if Anglos moved in. At this point, fate took charge. As a dejected Moses began his journey back home, he ran into an old friend, a renegade Dutchman born Philip Hendrik Nering Bogel, who had introduced himself to America under the fabricated title of the BARON DE BASTROP. Being a European and therefore more acceptable to the Spaniards than the crude Anglos (and a charmer to boot), he had soon made friends with the government of New Spain, and now set about persuading it to welcome his old friend Moses Austin. The Spanish agreed to make an exception to their anti-American rule and accept Moses' application.

In spite of frequent changes in government (Spain, the Republic of Mexico, the Empire of Mexico, a second Republic, and so forth), and the gut-wrenching but inevitable struggles caused by the cultural differences between the Anglo Americans and the Hispanics, the empresario system worked. Fired by a mixture of economics and mores, colonizers poured into empty terrain from states as near as Louisiana and as far away as Maine under the auspices of a determined group of American empresarios.

Mary Foster Hutchinson

The Anglican Mission - Part 1

The Latin Church had largely withdrawn. So where was the Anglican Church? Even as Texas was shaking off the heavy hand of Spain, English religion was approaching.

Among the inhabitants of an island once called Britannia were Christians who believed that their faith was inherited from the very first converts to carry Christianity outside the Holy Land. The Word, they believed, had arrived in their remote island in the first century on the lips of JOSEPH OF ARIMATHEA, in whose tomb Our Lord had been placed after the crucifixion. Joseph, they argued, could have derived his wealth from the tin trade centered in Cornwall. After the Ascension of Christ, what could have been more natural than for Joseph to share his new faith with the Britons?

Through wars and invasions and all sorts of turmoil, Britannia became England and Joseph's faith, later called the Anglican faith, survived, and was carried to America by the earliest Anglo explorers. The first service from *The Book of Common Prayer* conducted in the New World took place in 1577, when SIR FRANCIS DRAKE touched the coast of California during his famous voyage around the world on the *Golden Hind*. Soon after, the Church of Old England sent missionaries to the New World carrying the banner *"Transiens Adiuvanos"* (We Cross the Seas to Give Help). The first service of Holy Communion was conducted in 1607 in Jamestown, Virginia. From this illustrious ancestry, in due time, the Episcopal Church in the USA descended.

These crusaders brought with them to America the bones and flesh of their ancient church, set in all the glory and panoply of history. They called themselves Episcopalians because they believed that through bishops (*episcopus* in Latin) they were eternally linked to Jerusalem, even in the wilderness of a new world.

Bishops have always been the shepherds of orthodox Christendom. That's why they carry croziers, which represent stylized shepherds' crooks. During the Middle Ages, a bishop was considered to be of exalted rank, equal in majesty to a prince. As a sign of royalty, he was entitled to sit during an assembly, while others stood. Consequently, the church building where a bishop presided contained a special bishop's chair. Such a church became known as a cathedral church because it contained a *cathedra* (Greek for chair, or throne). In the serpentine way of languages, therefore, "chair" came to mean "leader." Even today, although everyone gets to sit down at meetings, the person in charge is still known as the Chair. And that is why we are not just St. Matthew's Church but St. Matthew's Cathedral Church. Our church contains the throne (*cathedra*) of the Bishop of Dallas.

The area of a bishop's jurisdiction was called a Diocese, or See (from a Latin word meaning seat). Since bishops were often away from their cathedrals on diocesan business, a clergyman called a dean was appointed to attend to the daily needs of local parishioners.

It was all a bit different from a lonely preacher on horseback carrying his private Gospel from settlement to settlement. But in a roundabout way, the Episcopal Church was approaching.

In the early 19th century an Episcopal priest named RICHARD S. SALMON caught the Texas fever. He thought he could move from New York to this savage place and take Anglicanism with him. His original idea had been to enter Texas as an accredited missionary, but the American Episcopal Church had a firm policy of never sending missions into foreign countries which already had an official religion. New Spain was Roman Catholic, and that was that. Still, the Rev. Mr. Salmon was determined. There were other ways to enter the Promised Land.

It is hard to exaggerate the almost rock-star notoriety which Texas enjoyed in the United States during this period. All over America, men gathered to hear the sales pitches skillfully thrown by agents of the empresarios. Austin Colony led the way, describing with practiced eloquence the beauty and fertility to be allotted, but failing to mention three digit heat or barbaric aborigines. Moses Austin had died soon after being awarded his empresario contract, but his place had been taken by his ambitious son Stephen, no mean salesman. The Rev. Mr. Salmon was one of STEPHEN F. AUSTIN's best customers. In 1836 he set out from New York with fifteen families and stars in his eyes to form an Episcopal colony in Texas.

His first stop was New Orleans, where an Episcopal parish had been established in 1804. There, bad news awaited. New Spain had won its independence from Old Spain, and changed its name to the Republic of Mexico. All colonization contracts awarded by the Spanish government were declared null and void. Would-be empresarios must now reapply for permission to establish colonies, an uncertain process which would take a leisurely path of months, if not years. Many disillusioned Episcopalians returned to New York. But the Rev. Mr. Salmon still followed his star, later serving as chaplain of the Republic of Texas Senate and presiding at the funeral of Stephen Austin, whose mother was an Anglican.

Sometimes it is necessary to build an altar in one place so that the fire from heaven may descend elsewhere. Richard Salmon's dream of an Episcopal colony died, but would not be forgotten.

Texas was, however, a strange place for an Episcopal priest to settle in. Unlike Louisiana, now enjoying religious freedom as part of the USA, Mexican Texas still required migrants to affirm membership in the Roman Catholic Church. The Rev. JOHN WURTZ CLOUD (who arrived in Texas in 1831 and kept a school in Brazoria) and his father, the Rev. ADAM CLOUD, had already endured the hurricanes, floods, cholera, heat, poverty, mud, drought, bandits, yellow fever, and blue northers which Texas had to offer. They had no realistic prospect of being able to practice their faith in any but the most secret way. What were they thinking?

Well, for one thing, all American immigrants, most of whom were Protestants, were assured that Mexico only required tacit

Holy Heritage

acceptance of Roman Catholicism and would not press the point. Indeed almost no R. C. priests were ever sent to Texas. In Mexican belief, crime discreetly hidden was excusable. Punishment was reserved for open transgressions. So long as the American settlers did not try to hold public Protestant services, no one cared what they believed.

And then of course our early Episcopal priests must have been pretty confident that there were better days ahead. Trusting that independence from Mexico and an eventual meld with the USA were inevitable, they laid their bets. Religious freedom in Texas must surely come, and come quickly.

They were right.

CHAPTER TWO
THE SETTLERS

A Feeble New Country

Although republicans throughout the world cheered as Mexico declared its independence from Spain in 1821, the infant nation proved incapable of sustaining a stable government. In 1822, the First Republic was discarded in favor of the imperial rule of Emperor Agustin I, which in 1824 gave way to the Second Republic, a federally based regime under whose auspices most early Anglo colonists entered Texas. By 1825, 800 "Catholic" American families had been granted six million acres of Texas land under the auspices of five American empresarios. All these grants covered land in south and central Texas. Indian-infested Northern Texas, including future Dallas, remained out of bounds.

Unfortunately, the enlightened Mexican government of 1824 soon gave way to petty dictatorships. Texas settlers became disenchanted by Mexico's political vacillation and confused by the contradictory and remote government of GENERAL SANTA ANNA. (This half-mad military genius had one of his legs - lost in combat - enshrined in a Mexico City park with full military honors.) By 1832, the English-speaking colonists were petitioning the Mexican government for local schools, local autonomy, and separate statehood. None of this was forthcoming.

The Texians, as these early settlers called themselves, hoped to return to the displaced liberal constitution of 1824. By 1836 many were convinced that this would never happen, and on March 2 the Texas Declaration of Independence was signed by sixty determined and outraged citizens. Among the reasons given for separation from the Mexican dictatorship was that *"It denies us the right of worshiping the Almighty according to the dictates of our own consciences by the support of a national religion calculated to promote the temporal interest of its human functionaries rather than the glory of the true and living God."* The General Convention of the Episcopal Church of the USA was now free to take Texas under its wing.

But first, a hierarchy had to be established. In 1838 the Rt. Rev LEONIDAS POLK, the first Episcopal Bishop to set foot in Texas, was consecrated Missionary Bishop of the Southwest, an immense area including the future Lone Star state. Although the Roman Catholic Church had theoretically dominated Texas religious life for three and a half hundred years, their first Texas bishop, JEAN MARIE ODIN, created bishop of Galveston in 1837, only beat us Texas Episcopalians to a place in the Apostolic Succession by one year.

Bishop Polk was quoted in The Episcopal Churchman of March/April 1977 as having identified infant Texas as a land where *"survival of the fittest was the law of the land, and where tough, rugged individualism was the secret of life."* Texas, he believed, *"was particularly open to the Episcopal Church where orderly, sober, and enlightened ministrations appealed to the transferred Anglo Americans, offering an anchor of stability in the midst of uncertainties, disorders, and hardships of life in that feeble new country."*

What a leap of faith!

Still, leapers were not long in coming. The Rev. CHARLES NEWELL, a Deacon of the Church, had been operating a school in Velasco as early as 1837, and returned to the USA to write a history of the new Republic the following year. People read it. The Revs. CALEB IVES and R. M. CHAPMAN became the first official missionaries of the Episcopal Church to the Republic. On

Christmas Day 1838, the first official service of Holy Communion according to the Book of Common Prayer was celebrated, defying outbreaks of yellow fever and cholera. In 1839 Christ Church Matagorda became the first official Episcopal parish in Texas.

The General Convention, though well aware of the plight of the many South Texas Episcopalians who remained without clergy, was hampered like every other institution by a lack of funds. It was not until 1841 that its members at last felt financially able to designate Texas (along with West Africa) as an official foreign mission field. (Texians familiar with West Africa could not have been flattered by this pairing.)

Three years later, in 1844, the Rt. Rev. GEORGE WASHINGTON FREEMAN of Newcastle, Delaware, became Second Missionary Bishop of the Southwest and First Provisional Bishop of Texas. He would welcome Saint Matthew's founder into the fold.

A Cultural Revolution

Except for its inclusion in large general maps, the first official record of that part of Texas which would eventually become Dallas occurred when the Republic of Texas divided itself into counties. Only South and Central Texas had enough official business to need county government, but in order to leave nothing to chance these early counties extended their boundaries north to the Red River. Robertson County, established in 1837 and named for Empresario STERLING ROBERTSON'S Colony (which was located along the Old Spanish Road near present day Bryan-College Station), encompassed half of present-day Dallas County, all of Tarrant County, most of Parker County, and a corner of Palo Pinto County. At the time, there was almost no one in the vicinity of future Dallas to know or care that their county seat, Franklin, lay 140 dangerous miles south. Before anyone could be found to protest, a cultural war had to be won.

At least one early visitor declared that if history is entitled to any credit, no immigrants ever suffered more than the first settlers of Texas. Sadly, the mores of the aborigines and that of the intruders were irreconcilable, and both sides knew it. The Lords of the Plains understood what was happening. They called the compass used by surveyors "the machine which steals our land." It was and it did. The Comanche did not surrender their hunting grounds gladly.

The farther north the plow came, the greater the risks to the settlers. In 1836 the Parker family, a group of Baptists, were farming near present day Groesbeck. Attacked by a group of Comanches, Kiowas, and Caddoes, five were murdered and mutilated, and seven kidnaped to become Comanche slaves, including CYNTHIA ANN PARKER, aged nine, who was forced to watch her grandmother being pinned to the ground by a Comanche spear and gang-raped.

In 1839 ANNETTE WHEELOCK was widowed in an Indian raid, and was informed that the victorious Indian chief had cut out her husband's heart and eaten it, hoping to absorb some of his valor. As a tribute, the chief sent the grieving widow two gifts, a powder horn and a proposal of marriage, which was declined. The dead hero was Annette's second husband, the father of her two children, both of whom had died in infancy. Her first husband had succumbed to an epidemic of Yellow Fever. At the time of her second widowhood, Annette had yet to reach her nineteenth birthday.

The settlement of North Texas was scarred with many such tragedies. Before Dallas could begin, one way of life had to decrease, one to increase. President SAM HOUSTON, raised by Cherokees, was unable to find a solution fair to both sides. In 1838 President MIRABEAU LAMAR, a believer in racial cleansing, used treaties and troops to work toward achieving a more or less Indian-free nation. To Americans, the settlement of North Texas began at last to seem tenable. Still, they faced substantial challenges.

In addition to the iniquity of man, nature had provided its own barriers. The Cross Timbers (an area stretching widely north and south but narrowly east to west, from the Red River almost to present day Waco) was described as almost impenetrable. To the west lay the Llano Estacado, the Staked Plains, where mere humans could disappear in the high grass stretching unbroken to the horizon, like some great heaving ocean. Navigable rivers, the super highways of the time, were few. The ability to obtain title to this empty land was clouded. When independence from Mexico had been declared, all empresario activity ceased. Soon enough, however, necessity revived the custom. The new Republic needed cash. A few European countries had acknowledged its sovereignty, but all refused pleas for loans. President Lamar reopened the profitable empresario system.

The Last Empresarios

WILLIAM SMALLING PETERS, an English-born military bandsman and music publisher living in Pennsylvania, thought immigration to Texas might prove attractive to the English middle class. As Bishop Polk had hoped, many newcomers might well be Anglicans, introducing an educated cadre into the raw republic. Peters' group of investors included his son, WILLIAM CUMMINGS PETERS, a mentor of composer Stephen Foster and a successful publisher of music in Louisville. Early in 1841, together with other investors, they signed the first of a total of four contracts with the Republic of Texas, authorizing them to settle a North Texas area covering an incredible ten million acres. It included future Dallas County, and was known as the Peters Colony.

The investors were to receive ten premium sections (a section equaled 640 acres) for every one hundred families settled. The settlers' shares were equally handsome. And once they had arrived in the Republic of Texas, they could not be pursued for any debts incurred back home. Even so, few Englishmen caught the Texas fever, possibly because the slave trade, abolished in England in 1833, was legal here. By 1844 only 197 families out of the 800 expected had arrived in what became known as Peters Colony. Additional Americans, mostly from Kentucky, eventually filled parts of this vast domain, but by that time, disenchanted and broke, William S. Peters had long ago withdrawn his support.

The Mercer Colony

General GEORGE FENTON MERCER, an investor in Peters Colony, thought he could do better. The Mercer Colony lay south and east of what is now the Metroplex and included 18 future counties including a part of Dallas County. General Mercer was a distinguished gentleman of unquestioned honor and probity, a Princeton College classmate of both John Marshall, later a Justice of the U. S. Supreme Court, and John Henry Hobart, later an Episcopal Bishop. What General Mercer did not know was that much of the huge acreage he had been legally awarded was already inhabited by squatters. A believer in the rule of law who placed unmerited confidence in the efficiency of Texas government, he was quite unable to cope with the tornado which awaited his honorable attempts to place his legal settlers.

In North Texas the Peters' and Mercer's Colonies and the whole system of empresario contracts had become intensely unpopular. All local sentiment favored the squatters. Technically, Colony agents had an authority that made them equal or superior to elected local officials. But the squatters would have none of it. Bloody riots erupted in the vicinity of future Dallas. By 1852 General Mercer had withdrawn, his dreams erased from Metroplex history except for the name of his sub-agent, a medical doctor called DANIEL ROWLETT, which was later adopted by a thriving suburb. Few know today why two thoroughfares in present-day Rockwall and Carrollton are called Peters Colony Road.

Holy Heritage

Peters and Mercer, both filled with the loftiest intentions, left behind bitter litigation which was not resolved until the mid nineteen thirties. So much had been planned, so much hoped for. What went wrong?

The Birth of a Village

Every settlement has its founder. Rome has Romulus and Remus. Dallas has JOHN NEELY BRYAN. Bryan built the iconic cabin on display in downtown Dallas in late 1841, after the region had already been allotted to Peters Colony. He was a lawyer and ought to have realized that squatting in itself wouldn't necessarily secure legal title to what was known as a headright. Official papers had to be filed. But not only did he stake out a large area for himself on his own authority, he also sold smaller sections to unsuspecting settlers. (His own land grant was not confirmed until 1854, still thirteen years in the future.) When Peters' and Mercer's clients arrived at their legally acquired acreage, they were met with angry residents who resisted with fists and firearms.

Some of these squatters had established themselves in their illicit cabins, growing crops, raising livestock, looking upon themselves as settlers. Legally established or not, they were outraged when confronted by newcomers carrying paper deeds for what they regarded as their own property. The holders of the deeds were equally outraged to find their grants already occupied by men they considered illegals. Both were victims of the early land laws of Texas, which were so convoluted that it was perfectly possible for the same tract of land to be legally claimed by as many as six "owners." There were plenty of lawyers, but most were, as a contemporary observer remarked, admirably qualified to make darkness visible. As we used to ask when I was young and played bridge on a dormitory floor, "Who dealt this mess?"

Born a Tennessean in 1810, scion of the wave of Scots who arrived in the American South in the 18th century carrying their

Presbyterian faith and their independent spirit with them, Bryan was educated at Fayetteville Military Academy and in private law offices. He started his adult life as a member of the Tennessee Bar.

After a severe bout of cholera, he spent some months (like Sam Houston) among the Cherokee, learning their language and customs. In 1833, he became an Indian trader in Arkansas. In 1839, seeking a new business site, he made his first trip to the spot which became Dallas, but it was not until late 1841 that he was settled on the east bank of the Trinity River, near what is now our business district.

He was not the first Anglo-American to explore this locality. In 1837 a group of mounted Texas Rangers on a scouting trip had camped at the mouth of what is now known as Turtle Creek. In 1840 five soldiers under Col. WM. G. COOKE had been killed by Indians nearby. But Bryan knew that the Republic of Texas Congress had recently authorized the construction of a military highway to connect Austin to the Red River. He foresaw that a community built on the spot where this artery crossed the Trinity would flourish.

A preliminary source of settlers was found in nearby Bird's Fort, located about 22 miles north of Bryan's cabin, where in 1839 Capt. JOHN BIRD and six other Texas Rangers died in a battle with 200 Comanches. Site of the signing of a peace treaty between the Republic of Texas and various Indian tribes, Bird's Fort was one of a series of garrisons established by the Austin government all the way to the Red River in an attempt to make settlement safe in north Texas. Most of its tiny population moved to Bryan's new community. JOHN BEEMAN, his wife and children, became Dallas' first permanent family, arriving in April of 1842 to plant the first corn. Like many, Beeman had found his paradise. *"Here I can drive a stake down,"* an early frontiersman boasted, *"to within 100 feet of where the Garden of Eden was located."*

Eden maybe, but the days of the Republic were drawing to a close. As many settlers had hoped and planned for, Washington was now turning a favorable eye toward the idea of adding Texas to the Union. In the prospective territory, a plebiscite was held. The population of Dallas voted 19 - 13 in favor of joining the US of A.

Washington dates the year of Texas' acquisition as 1845, when on the last day of December the US congress voted us in. But uniquely among all states, Texas became part of the USA by treaty, as an independent nation. This treaty required the approval of both legislative bodies. It was not until February 19, 1846, that the Republic of Texas legislature voted to draw down its Lone Star flag to become the 28th state in the USA. When an attempt was made to raise the US flag in its place, the pole splintered and fell to the ground. A second pole had to be provided for the Star Spangled Banner.

Bryan's little town grew, surviving the temporary absence in 1849 of most male citizens hoping to make their fortunes in the California gold rush. The fortunes of its founder were in decline. After giving up on the gold rush, Bryan wandered the west for four years before returning to his home on the Trinity and to his abandoned wife and children. In 1855, he disappeared again, a fugitive from the local sheriff after shooting a man who (he complained) had insulted his wife. This time his walkabout lasted for six years.

When the Civil War broke out in 1861, Bryan returned to Texas and joined Col. NICHOLAS D. DARNELL's Eighteenth Texas Cavalry, from which he was shortly discharged for medical reasons. This discharge offers a clue, perhaps, to his increasingly erratic behavior. By 1874 his mental state was described as "clearly impaired." In 1877 he was committed to the State Insane Asylum in Austin. He died there later the same year, and was buried in an unmarked grave.

However Bryan's private life may be deplored, his choice of a town site proved brilliant. As if foreseeing its future as a transportation hub, he placed it on an ancient Indian trail reaching from Mexico to Ohio, a section of which was about to be modernized as the Preston Trail. This early version of a superhighway led from Austin to the town of Preston on the Red River, now submerged under Lake Texoma. Preston Trail exists today as Preston Road, one of the busiest Dallas thoroughfares.

The future city of Dallas was set on a 300 - 500 feet thick deposit of Austin Chalk, still visible around town, especially around White Rock Lake, which was named for the formation. In the old days five yokes of oxen could hardly pull a plow through the region's dense, waxy, rich alluvial soil, which was admirable for farming.

But from the first, Dallas was destined to become urban, not rural. In 1844, inside the village limits, a surveyor named J. P. DUMAS drew a dream plan, a half mile square section of blocks and streets near the present day business district (but failing to allow for alleys, condemning downtown Dallas to decades of trash and congestion).

Along the river the village perched 512 feet above sea level. Although the Trinity was no Mississippi and its modest cliffs no Grand Canyon, Dallas was a good place to plant corn, to plant people, to plant a church. But at first no church came.

No one knows for sure the origin of the new settlement's name. Dallas is the surname of a small Scottish clan which can be traced back to the thirteenth century. Today it identifies a tiny ski resort in the Highlands. But Bryan is said to have declared that he called his village Dallas as a tribute to a friend, and there were two settlers named Dallas in the vicinity, either one of which might have been so honored.

In 1846, when our present-day county was formed, it seemed appropriate to borrow the name Dallas, already in use for three years by the area's principal town, while at the same time honoring GEORGE MIFFLIN DALLAS, vice president under U.S. President JAMES POLK. Both American politicians were popular in the Republic of Texas for favoring its admission by treaty into the

USA. The identical nomenclature for town and county was probably coincidental.

A Failed Paradise: The Rise and Fall of La Reunion

Dallas grew, being chosen as county seat in 1850, and in 1855 becoming home to a group of remarkable pilgrims, about 200 bedraggled idealists from France, Belgium, and Switzerland who arrived at the limestone bluff overlooking the village of Dallas to establish Utopia. Like us, they sought to fill an empty chamber of the heart. Like us, they were hoping to unravel the secret of the universe. They weren't just land hungry. They were immigrants of the spirit. They had walked 250 miles from the Port of Houston to their 2,000 acres, purchased for $7 an acre, on the West Fork of the Trinity three miles west of Dallas, their possessions lumbering behind them on ox carts. As disciples of French philosopher FRANCOIS FOURIER, they hoped to found an enlightened socialist society in the wilderness.

Although a few were farmers, most were skilled watch-makers, weavers, brewers, store-keepers, and musicians. The latter were an impressive group including a former musical director of the Paris Odeon Theater, several instrumentalists, and the leader of a singing society. They were to form the nucleus of Dallas' future devotion to Euterpe, the classical muse of music. With them came an organ, a piano, several flutes, and a selection of violins. They sang and they danced the *do-si-do* and they threw a party every other Sunday night open to the whole community, which caused a certain amount of angst among the Sabbath-keeping Americans. Their number increased to almost 400. But although they attempted to grow their own food, an invasion of grasshoppers and the unpredictable Texas weather defeated them, especially after a blizzard in 1856 froze the Trinity River and destroyed their crops. By 1860 they had given up their ideals and accepted incorporation into the town of Dallas.

La Reunion contributed to Dallas its first botanist and pharmacist, first butcher, first brewer, and first manufacturer (of carriages). The colonists' education, superior to that of most of the Anglo settlers, introduced a high quality of refinement into the infant town, and marked the beginning of Dallas as a cultural center. The site of their former settlement is now a carefully manicured industrial area. None of their buildings remain but an easy drive will bring you to their well-kept cemetery, off Fish Trap Road between Singleton Blvd and the Trinity River. Once there, it will seem appropriate to salute their courage and enterprise. Reunion Tower, in the Dallas business district, is a memorial to their passage.

They brought culture to Dallas. Did they bring faith?

Their religious position is unclear. They did not include a minister in their community. During the end of their experiment, a traveling Roman Catholic priest dropped by twice a year, but throughout most of the life of La Reunion, a priest of another persuasion, a transplanted European like themselves, highly educated and fluent in the French language, was summoned to marry young couples and baptize new-borns.

His name was George Rottenstein, and he was an Episcopalian.

Illustration by Margo Miller
THE REVEREND GEORGE ROTTENSTEIN
1802-1868
FOUNDER AND FIRST RECTOR OF SAINT MATTHEW'S

CHAPTER THREE
THE FOUNDERS

The Anglican Mission Part 2

GEORGE ROTTENSTEIN

GEORGE ROTTENSTEIN became the first full-time resident Christian minister in Dallas. He was born in 1802 into an old patrician family in Frankfort am Main, Hessen-Nassau, Prussia, and grew up in the unsettled and contentious Germany which followed the defeat of Napoleon. He and his wife, ELIZABETHA FREDERICKE HEYSER, had three sons: CARL (afterwards Charles), FRANZ, and EMIL GEORGE, all baptized in the Lutheran Church in Hamburg. The young family was forced for political reasons to flee to France, and then to Switzerland and England, where they were accepted in the highest society. In London George entered religious life as a golden-tongued Methodist preacher. But in spite of his welcome in Great Britain, he, like many Germans of his time, sought his destiny in America. In July, 1837, the Rottensteins arrived in New York on the SS *St. James*.

Six years later Rottenstein was teaching and studying at Randolph Macon College in Virginia, oldest Methodist college in America. In 1846 the family followed a significant German migration to Texas, where he and his son Charles preached and edited a Methodist newspaper, *The Texas Christian Advocate*, in

Houston. But God had other plans. In the early eighteen fifties, to his father's dismay, Charles left Methodism to become an Episcopal priest.

Hoping to show his son the error of his ways, George Rottenstein threw himself into the study of Anglican theology and history, with the result that he himself was thoroughly converted to the Episcopal Church and was confirmed and later ordained by the Rt. Rev. GE0RGE WASHINGTON FREEMAN, second Missionary Bishop of the Southwest and first Provisional Bishop of Texas. On June 1, 1854, Rottenstein was appointed a missionary priest to the Germans of San Antonio. He had found his true calling in the Anglican priesthood.

After serving in San Antonio (at that time populated by more Germans than either Hispanics or Anglos), he was transferred to Corsicana, moving on from there, after a destructive fire, to a remote village of 500 souls called Dallas. Weather during the year 1856 was exceptionally severe. A cyclone was reported in what is now Cedar Hill, a blizzard covered the region with snow in May, only to be followed by a drought, and in December a solid sheet of ice transfigured the Trinity. Nevertheless, in May of 1856 the Rev. Mr. Rottenstein would celebrate Dallas' first service according to *The Book of Common Prayer* and a week later its first service of Holy Communion. Shortly later the son and two daughters of a local judge would receive the rite of Baptism.

Although Dallas was already ten years old when the Rev. George Rottenstein arrived, it was still rough territory. Its few inhabitants drank raw whiskey and feasted on bison tongues, a delicacy soon to disappear as the astronomical herds were pushed west. Still, savages were no longer a menace, there was food on the table, and settlers were turning their thoughts to worship.

Since 1844 simple denominational gatherings, mostly Church of Christ, Presbyterian, and Methodist, had been held occasionally in area settlements. It was in nearby Farmers Branch that an itinerant Methodist minister preached the first Christian sermon in what would become Dallas County. In 1846, the Webb family set a small structure aside as a chapel on their rural farm. (Webb Chapel Road is still a busy Dallas thoroughfare.) But of settled Christian worship with a permanent resident pastor there was none.

Sad but true, in a frontier town someone always opened a newspaper before someone else planted a church. In 1849 Dallas' first newspaper began publication weekly under the name of the *Cedar Snag,* (a reference to the many logjams which clogged the Trinity River) and later changed to the more dignified *Dallas Herald.* In the same year the first of the land riots occasioned by the Peters Colony grants erupted. The 1850 federal census showed that the population of the county had risen to 2,743 people, 163 of whom lived in town, two being German and twelve British. There were also 207 slaves. Occupations listed included two lawyers, two doctors, two wagon makers, one inn keeper, and one tailor, but no clergyman.

An account of the indictments handed down by Dallas' first Grand Jury gives us a glimpse into county life. Fifty-one citizens were charged with gambling, four with assault, one with murder, and one with dueling. This jury also granted Dallas' first divorce, whereupon the foreman promptly married the appellant.

In 1856 Dallas was granted a town charter during the regular session of the Sixth Texas Legislature. Dr. SAMUEL B. PRYOR, an isolated Episcopalian, was elected its first mayor. The Episcopal Church had its first Dallas communicant and only awaited the arrival of a priest. Later that same year George Rottenstein rode his horse down to the river, crossed the Trinity on a ferry made of two canoes lashed together, mounted another horse, climbed the bluff, and filled the sacred needs of La Reunion.

Only twenty years after Texas had declared her independence from Mexico, the spiritual poverty of Dallas was about to be addressed.

The Dallas *Times Herald* reflected local excitement at the

prospect of housing a settled man of God. Its issue of May 24, 1856, contained the following notice:

> *Religious Notes:*
> *Protestant Episcopal Church:*
>
> *Rev. Mr. Rottenstein will perform Divine Services in Dallas on Sunday, May 25, at Eleven o'clock A. M. And at half past Four P. M.* A later issue read: *"Services will be held regularly in the old store house of Smith and Patterson on Main Street."*

His first recorded service took place on May 25, 1856, on the second floor of a vacant building on Main Street between Houston and Broadway (approximately where Dealey Plaza is today), with four attending, the celebrant, his wife, a Presbyterian woman named Mrs. Sarah Gray, and a Campbellite man, Col. Warren B. Stone. A wooden rail separated the chancel from the congregation. Two dry-goods boxes covered with orange calico formed the reading desk and the altar. Rottenstein had found his spiritual home, and Dallas its first permanent Christian minister. Somewhere angels were singing.

Sixteen months later, on September 21, 1857, the Feast Day of SAINT MATTHEW THE APOSTLE, formal Articles of Association were signed, establishing St. Matthew's as an official Parish. (We were allowed to skip the customary mission status.) In May, 1858, the rector and his wife journeyed to Austin, where the Articles were ratified by the Diocesan Council. St. Matthew's Parish now occupied a humble place in the world-wide Anglican Communion.

Holy Heritage

Why Saint Matthew?

Few things in life give more satisfaction than the art and privilege of naming. Few are more important. In the Second Chapter of the Book of Genesis we read …

So God formed out of the ground all the wild animals and all the birds of heaven. He brought them to the man (Adam) to see what he would call them, and whatever the man called each living creature that was its name.

The animals now had identity. They had names. These did not serve only as labels. Many of our ancestors believed that whoever knows your name has control over you. (Remember Rumpelstiltskin and the second act of *Turandot*?) Everyone agrees that names carry power. And consequences. Psalm 91, verse 14 reads - "*I will set him on high because he hath known my Name.*"

When the Rev. Mr. George Rottenstein established St. Matthew's Parish in the tiny town of Dallas that September he had a choice of days. Look at the liturgical calendar. A bit earlier, and our parish could have been dedicated to Saint Bartholomew; a bit later, to St. Michael. Was the choice of St. Matthew an accident? Or was it planned? Matthew means "Gift of God." The saint himself, a former tax collector, was one of the Twelve, and a witness both to the Resurrection and the Ascension. He was literate in Aramaic, his birth tongue, and Greek, the language of the market place. It was at his banquet table that Our Lord announced that he had come to call sinners, not the righteous, to redemption. Little is known of Matthew's later life, although some traditions hold that he preached to the Jews, perhaps evangelizing later in Ethiopia, perhaps dying a martyr.

What link did he have to the Rottensteins' Germany, or to Dallas, in the nineteenth century? There was an ancient Scottish belief that St. Matthew's skull had been preserved in medieval times at Rosslyn Chapel near Edinburgh. Immigrants from Scotland may have sought to bring the saint's protection and favor to Texas with them but, if so, any record of their influence has been long forgotten, as has any possible connection with the Scottish Clan called Dallas.

To Christendom at large, Saint Matthew was best known as the author of the first Synoptic Gospel. In art which depicts Matthew, Mark, Luke and John symbolically as the four living creatures of Revelation 4:7, he is represented by the form of a winged man. He is the patron saint of accountants, bankers, tax collectors, bookkeepers, and (of course) our parish. His symbol is a group of money bags. Was this a harbinger of things to come? Or was our founder focusing on Matthew the winged man when he chose our patron? Wings have always been a symbol of spiritual ascent. Or perhaps the fateful parish meeting at which our parish was first voted into being just happened to fall on St. Matthew's Day by chance.

Unexpectedly, the new clergyman (brought up let us remember as a son of minor European nobility) fell in love with Dallas. Poor and tiny as his congregation was, Rottenstein worked untiringly for it and shared its hopes for the future. Even knowing what was to come, we might have found it hard to identify that muddy huddle of shacks as the seed of a great metropolis, but to its first citizens the future looked bright. By 1860 Dallas had achieved a population of 1,800, thirty stagecoach lines charging ten cents a mile for the two days' trip to Waco, a barber shop, two hotels, musical soirees, seven merchants' houses, two stables, a brick yard, two blacksmiths, two schools, and a musical society.

It all happened very quickly. St. Matthew's Episcopal Parish was flourishing in its rented rooms, but responding to the pace of the times, the parishioners soon grew tired of orange calico reading desks. There was a strong feeling that a church wasn't a real church until it had a building of its own. But construction costs money, which was scarce in the country at large, and almost non-existent in Dallas. Eventually, the rector, despairing of local fund raising, offered to take himself and his wife to Louisiana where he could find a parish to support them while St. Matthew's deposited his Dallas salary in a building fund.

It was a gallant offer, but it is probably just as well that no church had been built by July 6, 1860, when (with the thermometer standing unofficially at 106 degrees F), a disastrous fire raged through the Dallas business district. This area and many residential houses were total losses, made worse by the suspicion that arson had been committed by local slaves, egged on by abolitionist preachers recently arrived from Iowa. The preachers were expelled from the town and several slaves were hanged. Whether the victims were guilty or innocent (there is evidence on both sides), it was not Dallas' finest hour. And the War Between the States was just around the corner.

A Birthday into Heaven

Only a year after Dallas' Great Fire, another disaster rocked the infant parish of St. Matthew.

On June 8, 1861, a state of civil war was declared, and the town of Dallas voted to secede from the USA to join the Rebel cause. Far from the hostilities, Dallas was nevertheless important as one of eleven quartermaster and commissary posts for the Trans-Mississippi Army of the Confederacy. Like Dallas, the Rottensteins were loyal Confederates. The Rev. Mr. Rottenstein immediately volunteered to be a Confederate Army chaplain for the duration, and one of his sons joined the ranks.

The war was hard on Dallas and St. Matthew's. Bishop Freeman had been succeeded by the Rt. Rev. JAMES ALEXANDER GREGG, created first bishop of Texas in 1859, who made two visitations during hostilities from his headquarters on the Gulf coast and managed to keep his tiny Dallas congregation on life support. An Englishman, the Rev. Dr. STEPHEN MCKAYE, who was working toward his ordination to the priesthood, served as interim rector. Throughout the war, J. H. PATTERSON, the senior warden, never failed to send a diocesan report every year, including the parish assessment of $5, paid out of his own pocket.

When the war ended in 1865, Dr. McKaye retired to England and the rector was at last able to return to his beloved Dallas, where he and his wife moved into the old Keaton Hotel, on the corner of Jefferson and Commerce. He was badly needed. Texans felt humiliated, defeated, and bitter, attributes which would linger.

At first, services were held in the auditorium of the courthouse, across the street from the hotel. When that refuge proved too cold in the winter, the congregation moved to a hall over a small brick store on the corner of Main and Jefferson (where the Records Building now stands) for a rent of $12 a month. Although Rottenstein's health had been broken by the privations of war, he had not forgotten his peoples' yearning for a permanent home and was able to raise $1,000 toward a church building he would never see.

This devoted and sanctified man, revered by all who knew him, entered into eternal life in February 1868, consecrating the Elements of his own Last Communion. He died reciting the *Gloria*.

He was buried in the City Cemetery, and in the absence of any other Christian minister in the community, his funeral was conducted according to the rites of the Masonic Order, of which he was a member. His obituary read, *"Largely endowed by nature with a brilliant intellect, enriched by cultivation of the highest order, a ripe scholar and devoted Christian, the Church ever found in him an able defender and exponent of its doctrines."*

In 1941 a local newspaper wrote of him that the celebration of his life was an occasion for proud and grateful review of achievement in which the entire city should join. In 1952 St. Matthew's parishioners dedicated a memorial stone on the grave of their first priest, founder of their parish, and father of the Episcopal Church in North Texas. At a later time, his body was translated to the altar of the Orand Chapel (now St. Nicholas Church) in Flower Mound.

George Rottenstein deserves to be honored by the City of Dallas as its first permanent resident Christian minister, by us as our Spiritual Father, our Founder, and (if we believe that a life of devotion unto death is equal to the physical sacrifice of that life) as our Proto Martyr.

II. THE BOOK OF MINISTERS

IN ITS ONE HUNDRED AND FIFTY-EIGHT YEARS,
FIRST AS A PARISH CHURCH,

THEN AS A CATHEDRAL,

SAINT MATTHEW'S HAS BEEN LED

BY

ONE FOUNDING RECTOR,

    NINETEEN DEANS,

        AND NINE BISHOPS.

WHO WERE THESE HALLOWED MEN?

THE APOSTLE OF TEXAS
THE MOST REVEREND ALEXANDER CHARLES GARRETT
1832-1924
FIRST BISHOP OF DALLAS
AND 14TH PRESIDING BISHOP OF THE EPISCOPAL CHURCH

CHAPTER FOUR
A DIGNITY OF BISHOPS

We have seen that our religion has been carried through the centuries by men called bishops, set aside to guard and transmit the Faith, and that each bishop has been placed in charge of an area called a diocese, made up of a family of individual churches called parishes. Before the American Revolution, parishes in America fell under the jurisdiction of the Bishop of London, and shared his cathedral church of St. Paul's.

After independence, our new nation acquired its own bishops, but at first they avoided founding cathedrals, which were considered undemocratic. It was not until 1850 that the Diocese of Chicago established the first American cathedral church, but soon Episcopalians came to recognize the importance of cathedrals as symbols of the nobility and beauty of our worship. Remote dioceses, however, covering several states and territories, were supervised by remote bishops. Many of these pioneer bishops considered the areas they had to administer too vast for such a system to be practical. In the wilderness, cathedrals had to wait.

A diocesan bishop is elected by the diocesan convention to serve as the chief pastor and shepherd of the diocese. Here is a list of all the bishops who, in their various guises, have assumed responsibility for the spiritual welfare of our bit of the world.

- The Rt. Rev. Leonidas Polk 1838 - 1843
  First Missionary Bishop of the Southwest.
- The Rt. Rev. George Washington Freeman 1844 - 1858
  Second Missionary Bishop of the Southwest and First Provisional Bishop of Texas.
- The Rt. Rev. James Alexander Gregg 1859 -1873
  First Bishop of Texas.
- The Most Rev. Alexander Charles Garrett 1874 - 1924
  First Missionary Bishop of North Texas, First Bishop of Dallas, and 14th Presiding Bishop of the Episcopal Church.
- The Rt. Rev. Harry Tunis Moore 1924 -1945
  Second Bishop of Dallas.
- The Rt. Rev. Charles Avery Mason 1945 - 1970
  Third Bishop of Dallas.
- The Rt. Rev. Archibald Donald Davies 1970 - 1983
  Fourth Bishop of Dallas.
- The Rt. Rev. Donis Dean Patterson 1983 - 1992
  Fifth Bishop of Dallas
- The Rt. Rev. James Monte Stanton 1993 - 2014
  Sixth Bishop of Dallas.

There are also two kinds of assistant bishops. Suffragan bishops (the word means "to give a vote of support"), of which we have had six, serve as assistants to their bishops and have no right of succession. Bishops coadjutor succeed automatically to the position of diocesan bishop on the resignation of their predecessors. Harry Tunis Moore was bishop coadjutor from 1917 - 1924, during the declining years of Bishop Garrett, whom he succeeded. Charles Avery Mason was bishop coadjutor under Moore from 1945-46, and followed him to the bishopric. All our bishops of whatever rank assumed the honorific of "Right Reverend" except Garrett, in his latter years. Rising to top rank, the office of Presiding Bishop of the Protestant Episcopal Church of the United States of America in 1924, he was addressed as "Most Reverend."

A Firm Foundation

The Church cannot survive without bishops because they furnish our link through the Apostolic Succession to the original apostles, but for the first eighteen years of St. Matthew's life, North Texas made do without either dean or cathedral. It was not until 1874 that the newly consecrated Bishop Garrett, carrying the ancient tradition with him from his native Ireland, named Dallas his see city and St. Matthew's his cathedral, giving us our first dean.

Here in Texas, "dean" was a confusing title. There are several kinds of deans. Deans may be teachers who run colleges, people who have held office in their organizations longer than any other members, officials in a monastery, or, as in the case of Saint Matthew's, persons in charge of the day-to-day operation of cathedrals while bishops attend to their dioceses.

The word "dean" descends from a Latin Vulgate word, *decamus*, meaning a person in charge of ten other persons, like a noncommissioned officer in an army. (*Decem* is the Latin word for ten.) It traveled through Old French, where it was spelled *deiem*, into Middle English, where it became *deen*. At first, it stood for the chief of a small group of monks (a chapter) in a monastery. As the number of churches increased and the great cathedrals were built, the word was borrowed to fill a more specific need.

How grand it all sounds! How could there ever be any such thing as a cathedral or an ecclesiastical prince called a bishop in the future of that burnt-out village called Dallas? This is how it happened.

LEONIDAS POLK, the Fighting Bishop

When independence from Mexico first made it possible to elect an Episcopal bishop to cover its massive territory, Texas was still pretty much a mystery to the General Convention back east. It seemed appropriate to bundle the new republic up with other huge and largely unknown western territories. As we have seen, in 1838 the Rt. Rev. LEONIDAS POLK, second cousin of US President James Polk, became the first man to exercise episcopal authority over Texas. But Texas formed only a part of his jurisdiction. As Missionary Bishop of the Southwest, his province included not only Texas but also the whole state of Arkansas and most of the Indian Territory which would one day become Oklahoma.

The Fighting Bishop, as he was called, was born in 1806 in Raleigh, North Carolina, into a prominent family, and educated at the University of North Carolina at Chapel Hill and West Point, where he was converted to the Episcopal Church and baptized in the presence of the entire corps of cadets. He later resigned his Army commission to study for the priesthood at Virginia Theological Seminary. He was ordained in 1831, and married Frances Devereux of Raleigh. He was a founder of the University of the South at Sewanee, Tennessee, served as Missionary Bishop of the Southwest from 1838 to 1841, and became the first Bishop of Louisiana. After the outbreak of the Civil War, his military training and devotion to his home state led him to set aside his ecclesiastical robes to become a general in the Confederate Army. He was killed in action in 1864 at the Battle of Marietta, and is buried in Christ Church Cathedral in New Orleans.

GEORGE WASHINGTON FREEMAN, the Provisional Bishop

Polk was succeeded as Missionary Bishop of the Southwest by the Rt. Rev. GEORGE WASHINGTON FREEMAN. Bishop Freeman was born in Sandwich, Massachusetts, in 1789, into a family of Puritan background. He became a professor at the Academy in New Bern, North Carolina, where friendship with Bishop Ravenscroft of North Carolina led him to be confirmed in the Episcopal Church, and to be ordained to the priesthood in 1827. He received the Doctor of Divinity Degree in 1839 from the University of North Carolina and served churches in that state, Tennessee, New Jersey, and Delaware. In 1844, after being rector of Emmanuel Church, Newcastle, Delaware, he was consecrated bishop in St. Peter's Church, Philadelphia.

His headquarters was in Little Rock, Arkansas, from which he traveled, mostly on horseback, to all parts of that state, Indian Territory, and the Republic of Texas, over which he was given provisional jurisdiction. He presided at the first recorded instance of confirmation in what is now the Diocese of Dallas, and it was he who mentored and confirmed George Rottenstein. He later became Bishop of Arkansas. He died in 1858 and is buried in Mount Holly Cemetery, Little Rock.

JAMES ALEXANDER GREGG, the Dixie Bishop

We now come to the first bishop who took immediate notice of Dallas and whose jurisdiction was (finally) wholly within the new state of Texas. JAMES ALEXANDER GREGG was born in Society Hills, South Carolina, to a Baptist family and was graduated from South Carolina College in 1838. He read law in Cheraw, South Carolina, and was admitted to the bar in 1841. In Cheraw he married Charlotte Wilson Kolloch, a devout Episcopalian, and under her influence was soon baptized and confirmed into the church. Ordained priest in 1847 after private study with BISHOP CHRISTOPHER E. GADSDEN, he became Rector of St. David's, Cheraw, which was to be his only parochial appointment.

As population grew in the Southwest, individual states attained diocese status, and this devout and kindly man, supported by independent means and a rugged physique, was chosen to become first bishop of Texas. He served until 1873, during George Rottenstein's rectorship at St. Matthew's.

Throughout the Civil War, in the absence of Rector Rottenstein (who was serving as a Chaplain in the Confederate Army), Bishop Gregg kept St. Matthew's alive. W. L. MURPHY, in his account of the early history of the Episcopal Church in Dallas, (as recorded by KENNETH FOREE in the *Dallas Morning News* of December 12,

1947), left us a vivid picture of one of his episcopal visits. Our town was still struggling to recover from the disastrous fire of 1860 and was condemned by many (including Bishop Gregg) as unhealthy, a sinkhole of malaria and bad water. Many of the 2,000 inhabitants were still living in tents and lean-tos. Few had ever seen a bishop. The news of his imminent arrival was galvanizing. Foree wrote:

> *It was to a stricken town that a bishop was coming. The Rt. Rev. Alexander Gregg, first and newly consecrated Bishop of Texas, was the man. He arrived here on Oct. 12, 1860, in a carriage pulled by two fine bays, driven by a Negro coachman, and accompanied by his chaplain, the Rev. Mr. QUIMBY. It was announced that he would conduct evening prayers and confirmation that night at the Masonic Hall. The town turned out. Before the time of the service Masonic Hall was choked by Methodists, Baptists, members of the Church of Christ, Presbyterians, and half a dozen or more Episcopalians, including the Mayor.*

What better proof do we have that Dallas, the future buckle on the Bible Belt, was thirsting to hear the word of God? And maybe eager to learn what manner of man a real live bishop could be.

But alas! This particular Bishop was being wined and dined by JUDGE J. M. PATTERSON, the senior warden of the parish, and was late in arriving. The assembly grew restless. Into the void stepped Brother MARLIN THOMPSON, accustomed to opening Methodist meetings with song. He stood to attention, quieted the room-buzz, and began with John Newton's *"How Tedious and Tasteless the Hours, When Jesus No Longer I See."* He sat down. Everyone waited again. Still no bishop.

The few Episcopalians present felt chagrined. It had not been until after the American Revolution that hymn singing had been authorized in Episcopal churches and this lusty practice still made many traditional Anglicans wince. But Methodist Thompson knew his job. After another silent interval, he stood up again and this time rendered a white spiritual *"If I Could Read My Title Clear to Mansions in the Sky."* Satisfied that he had done his best, he sat down. Everyone waited. Still no bishop. The congregation was beginning to squirm. Thompson stood up, and treated his captive audience to *"What a Friend We Have in Jesus,"* another good old Methodist hymn. Still no bishop.

By this time the Episcopalians were livid. This was supposed to be an Episcopal service. The later the bishop, the more Thompson sang, and the more the Episcopalians boiled. This was not the way their hallowed liturgy was supposed to commence. Tempers flared.

Mr. Foree continues.

> *Blood was on the moon, sacred services were about to dissolve into a riot, when there was a flutter. "The Bishop! The Bishop!" From a curtained corner issued the robed Bishop and his assistant in their vestments. "Aaaaaah" said a Dallas which had never seen the like.*

It never had. But it would many times again. Pioneer people were strongly attracted to the mystery, the beauty, and the sense of permanence of the Episcopal rite. Bishop Gregg, the official record reads, held brief services at the Masonic Hall to overflow crowds. Dallas was overwhelmed. It was a portent of times to come.

ALEXANDER CHARLES GARRETT,
the Bishop - Presiding Bishop

In 1874, the Diocese of Texas, having been judged too vast for one Bishop, was split into three dioceses, and ALEXANDER CHARLES GARRETT became the first Missionary Bishop of

North Texas. No one knew it yet, but a giant had entered the land. For close to fifty years his remarkable career illuminated both church and city.

Garrett was born in Ballymote, County of Sligo, Ireland, in 1832, the youngest of a family of sixteen which had produced Anglican clergy for generations. His father, grandfather, and great-grandfather had served as the priest in his home village for the previous 150 years. He was graduated from Trinity College, Dublin, where he received his divinity degree in 1855, was ordained priest in 1857, and married Letitia (Letty) Hope, the shy daughter of a prominent Dublin attorney. After serving as a curate in Hampshire, England, from 1856 to 1859, he spent ten years as a missionary in British Columbia, Canada, after an amazing seven-month voyage from Southampton and around Cape Horn to Victoria with his wife and two small children. In 1870 he emigrated to the United States and became Rector of St. James Church, San Francisco, and in 1872 Dean of Trinity Cathedral, Omaha, Nebraska.

Having been appointed Bishop of the Missionary District of North Texas in 1875 by the General Convenion, Garrett named our little town his see city and St. Matthew's his cathedral.

"I have adopted Dallas as my See city, Saint Matthew's Church therein as my Cathedral, and in the Name of our God I have set up my banner and grounded my staff, that the enemy may not prevail."

His letter to the parish reads in part *"St. Matthew's is henceforth to be called a cathedral because the Bishop's chair of office is to be there. Here is to be his ecclesiastical home, refreshed here he will go forth to his lonely journeys and carry still with him the impulse and momentum which his zeal and love have acquired in this spiritual center of life and peace.*

Here, as at a central heart, must the warm glow of spiritual life be ever maintained and the sweet harmony of an able ministry, a beautiful ritual, and profound purity be found. As the mother church thereof your interest, sympathy and aid must not be limited to yourselves alone, but must extend to every member of the family, no matter how remote his dwelling."

Thus, magically, our first church became our cathedral, and the raw community called Dallas a cathedral city. Has any forlorn and wounded community received a more glorious challenge?

Like George Rottenstein, Alex Garrett developed a deep affection for his adopted country. An unknown biographer recorded the following anecdote. Garret was on a fund-raising tour in *Philadelphia, when introduced to a large assembly by a noted layman of the city in this way. "I have visited Texas myself. I consider it the most God forsaken country on the face of the earth. I hope you will give the poor Bishop, who by the cruelty of the Church is expected to reside there, a patient hearing and a generous response." Garret replied "It is true my friends that we have some undesirable citizens in Texas, but we are catching them as fast as we can and sending them back to the various states of the Union in which they received their early training. My friend need not be alarmed, all who belong to him will return in due time."* Not too many people got ahead of Alex Garrett.

"Ride Like Cowboys, Pray Like Saints"

It was a Herculean task that this ardent Irishman undertook. His new diocese consisted of 100,000 square miles, three small frame buildings, (in Dallas, Paris, and Cleburne), and 360 communicants. Typically, he set about it with a will, beseeching seminaries in the east to send him *"clergy who could ride like cowboys, pray like saints, preach like apostles, and, having food and raiment, be therefore content."* Somehow, they were sent.

Noted for his down to earth nature, his unselfishness, and his astounding physical stamina, he was called the golden-tongued Chrysostom of the American Church for his eloquence. He became a well known author, and in 1897 represented St. Matthew's at the world-wide Lambeth Conference in Canterbury, which had recently adopted the Lambeth Quadrilateral, defining the four cornerstones of the Anglican faith as the Bible, the Creeds, the Sacraments, and the Episcopate. While in England, he was an honored guest of Queen Victoria at the 60th anniversary of her accession. At age 91 he became one of the first American clerics to broadcast his sermons on radio, and the oldest bishop in the worldwide Anglican Communion.

In 1923, during the last year of his eventful life, age 93 and totally blind, he ascended to the highest position possible in the American Episcopal Church as 14th Presiding Bishop, equal to an English Archbishop. The national House of Bishops met in Dallas for the only time that year. He died in office in 1924, lying in state at St. Mary's College before his cathedral obsequies. The Mayor of Dallas called for a minute of silence throughout the city at noon on the day of his funeral. He is buried at Oakland Cemetery in Dallas. Ten deans served our cathedral during his tenure.

From the beginning, the "Apostle of Texas" could have no illusions about his new flock. His first duty upon arriving in Dallas on New Year's Eve, 1874, was to officiate at the funeral of a man mortally shot in a saloon brawl. The Rt. Reverend Bishop, however, never abandoned his British roots. Like George Rottenstein, Garrett came out of the top drawer. The arts of cautioning parishioners against stamping their feet during his sermons and refraining from spitting on the floor of the sanctuary cannot have been part of the curriculum in Dublin. He had to improvise.

But Alex Garrett was a quick learner. Well-hardened by the brutal mission life he had led in Canada, he adapted, giving praise where it was due, as when his flock built a fence around the church to keep out aggressive hogs. Anglican to the core, his innate dignity, gentleness, and nobility of mind earned him the respect and eventually the devotion of his rough congregation. He played no mean part in the civilizing of Dallas.

Although he was known as an author, his particular dedication was to the education of women. St. Mary's College, which he founded in 1889, was remarkable for its time and place, offering bachelor's and master's degrees to both local young ladies and boarders, of whom one, CLAUDIA TAYLOR, later became LADY BIRD JOHNSON, first lady of the United States. Sadly, the Bishop's wife remained a recluse in Dallas as she mourned the loss of their only daughter, kidnaped by Indians in British Columbia and never recovered. Letitia Garrett died in 1909, after fifty-five years of marriage. The couple was survived by one son, Henry, a gifted musician and engineer, who laid the foundation for WRR, the world's first municipal radio station, and invented an automobile which was fueled with water.

Bishop Garrett built 54 churches during his tenure, opened the eyes of the Eastern Seaboard to the needs of the Church in the west, and captivated the great and humble. When he died, the outpouring of love was universal.

HARRY TUNIS MOORE, Dean, Coadjutor, and Bishop

HARRY TUNIS MOORE had been Dean of St. Matthew's Cathedral for eleven years (1906-1917) when he was chosen to be Bishop Coadjutor to Bishop Garrett. On Garrett's death in 1924, he automatically became 2nd Bishop of Dallas. Altogether, he served us for nearly forty years.

To many, this period remains the high point of episcopal history in Dallas. For the first time I can now tell you, gentle readers, that I knew some of the august personages in our past. In 1949 an elderly Bishop Moore officiated at the wedding of my sister, under the nervous eye of the family, who were aware of his approaching senility. There was a story going around, perhaps apocryphal, that when called to conduct a similar ceremony he had been discovered opening the Prayer Book not to Holy Matrimony but to the Burial Office, and had to be gently refocused. Nothing of the sort occurred in my sister's case, much to the relief of the bridegroom's parents, who had been joined in wedlock by Bishop Moore twenty-eight years earlier.

During the seventeen years when as Bishop Coadjutor he assisted the fabled Bishop Garrett, Moore must have been in an unassailable position to absorb the devotion and energy of his legendary superior. With him, Moore watched the gentle decline of St. Mary's College, and when the diocese was in financial peril during the Great Depression engineered the sale of parish lands to keep the ecclesiastical head above water.

Tolerant and intelligent, Bishop Moore initiated Episcopal outreach to local colleges and endured the anxious years of the nineteen thirties and the double crisis of World War I (the War to End All Wars), and World War II, which proved the emptiness of that optimistic slogan. And he watched Dallas, now the center of banking, insurance, and fashion retailing for the Southwest, as it grew from a population of 90,000 to almost half a million inhabitants.

Famous for his wry wit, he was fond of saying,"*You can tell what the Lord thinks of money by looking at some of the people He gives it to.*" In 1945 Bishop Moore retired due to ill health, leaving the diocese with forty parishes and almost ten thousand communicants. He died in Dallas in 1955 after a long illness, and is buried in Grove Hill Memorial Park.

CHARLES AVERY MASON, - the Cornerstone Bishop

Bishop Mason literally worked himself to death. He oversaw one of the most phenomenal periods of missionary expansion in the history of the Episcopal Church. His aim was to find a place for every communicant in parish life and a parish for every neighborhood, made comfortable by the installation of a new-fangled device called an air conditioner. He almost did it.

Elected in 1945 as Coadjutor to Bishop Moore, whom he succeeded in 1946, CHARLES AVERY MASON was born in St.

Louis, Missouri, in 1904, to Charles Henry Mason and Mary Avery. He received his B.A. from Washington University in St. Louis and was a graduate of Virginia Theological Seminary, afterwards serving in churches in Washington, D.C., Illinois, New York City, and Staten Island, New York. He and his wife, Virginia, born in England to a British mother and Canadian father, had two daughters.

Mason increased the number of active Episcopalians in the Diocese of Dallas to 48,000 during his bishopric of 24 years, establishing almost 100 missions. To Bishop Mason, any old building represented the promise of a new church. St. John's started life as an abandoned chicken barn near White Rock Lake. St. Nicholas Flower Mound grew out of the Bishop Mason Retreat Center. His zeal led to the establishment of a Diocesan Center, and St. Philip's School and Community Center in a black neighborhood of Oak Cliff.

The city grew along with the diocese. During Mason's tenure Dallas became the place where future Nobel Laureate Jack Kilby of Texas Instruments invented the integrated circuit, making modern life possible, and where a population of 400,000 ballooned to about a million.

In 1946 Bishop Mason was awarded the degree of Doctor of Divinity by Virginia Theological Seminary and in 1948 he attended the Lambeth Conference at Canterbury. While in England, he represented Texans who had contributed steel for its rebuilding as Elizabeth the Queen Mother laid the cornerstone of the new All Hallows Church in London. This ancient parish, founded in the year 675 AD and the oldest in England, already had American connections. William Penn had been baptized there, after his father saved the venerable building from destruction during the Great London Fire of 1666. Unfortunately, twentieth century parishioners had been unable to save it from annihilation by Nazi bombers during the blitz.

Bishop Mason, godfather to fifty new parishes, died in office in 1970 and is buried in Hillcrest Cemetery.

ARCHIBALD DONALD DAVIES - THE SCHISMATIC BISHOP

ARCHIBALD DONALD DAVIES, a man who stood by his beliefs, was born in Pittsburgh, Pennsylvania, in 1920 to Archibald Davies, who designed blast furnaces for the steel mills. He was educated at the University of Tulsa and Western Theological Seminary and married Mabel Roberts in 1939. The couple had five children. After a period as instructor at Huron College and the University of Tulsa, he received the degree of Doctor of Divinity at Western and was ordained in 1950.

He served as Rector of St. Paul's in Manhattan, Kansas, and as Chaplain of Kansas State University. In 1954 he joined the Army Reserve as a chaplain and from 1962 - 64 was on active duty at Fort Hood. He also served as a fellow in the Adult Division of the Department of Education of the National Church and was a Professor of Pastoral Theology at Seabury Western. In 1956 he became Rector of Christ Church, Monroe, Louisiana, and in 1968 Dean of Trinity Cathedral, Omaha. There he became intrigued by the diaries of his predecessor, Alexander Garrett, and was responsible for their publication.

In 1970, following in Garrett's footsteps, he became the second Dean of Trinity Cathedral, Omaha, to become Bishop of Dallas. Davies saw his job as a chance to deepen religious awareness, in a place which, he thought, *"while visibly religious, may in fact wear its religion on its sleeve."* He worked hard to raise the influence of the church, introduced computers to the diocese, and was responsible for building our apartment home for the elderly, Cathedral Gardens. He oversaw the completion of Camp Crucis, and carried on the development of the Bishop Mason Center with its mausoleum, Garrett House, and chapel. He was a supporter of the Cursillo movement and began the establishment of the local Anglican School of Theology. He cheered on the Episcopal School of Dallas.

His tenure encompassed the publication of the 1979 edition of *The Book of Common Prayer*, and it fell to him to ease the adoption of its changes. A fellow of the College of Preachers in Washington, D.C., Davies was hailed as a "Shepherd of Souls," responsible for the consolidation and stabilization of the diocese within the catholic tradition of the Anglican Communion.

But he did not confine his influence to the existing structure. He was especially aware of the needs of have-nots, the poor in Dallas and elsewhere in the world. He helped to resettle 10,000 Southeast Asian immigrants in North Texas.

During his tenure, the number of Hispanics in the congregation grew to 500, and our Spanish speaking services were inaugurated, led by a distinguished succession of priests: the Rev. William Muniz, the Rev. Ron Robertson, the Rev. Uriel Osnaya, the Rev. Juan Jimenez, the Rev. Gerald Krumenacher, and the Rev. Canon Antonio Muñoz, the congregation's present incumbent.

While all this was going on, the population of North Texas was exploding, and the Diocese of Dallas, deemed too large for comfortable administration, was divided in two. In 1983, Davies left Dallas to become the first Bishop of the new Diocese of Fort Worth. There he was responsible for the forming of a corporation for the stewardship of property in the new diocese, taking property out of the hands of the bishop. He retired in 1985 to became Bishop of the Convocation of American Churches in Europe, serving until 1989 and developing a personal friendship with Pope John Paul II.

These were the years of change for the national church, many of which were opposed by Bishop Davies, a staunch upholder of conservative standards. After PECUSA adopted practices he considered incompatible with traditional Anglicanism, he left it to found a continuing Anglican church, the Christian Episcopal Church of America and Canada, of which he was primate.

He died in Granbury, Texas, in 2011 at the age of 91.

Mary Foster Hutchinson

DONIS DEAN PATTERSON, the Transitional Bishop

DONIS DEAN PATTERSON guided the Diocese of Dallas through the painful period of reorganization after its western portions became the Diocese of Fort Worth, and during introduction of the 1979 Book of Common Prayer and ordination of women to the priesthood. He ordained the first woman priest in the diocese, and at the time of his resignation there were five female priests in his jurisdiction.

Born in Holmesville, Ohio, in 1930, he was educated at Ohio State University. Commissioned in the Army, he served as a line officer in the Eighth Army Division in Korea, where he was confirmed in the Episcopal Cathedral of St. Mary and St. Nicholas in Seoul. Called to the ministry, he was trained at Harvard and the Episcopal Theological School in Cambridge, Massachusetts, from which he received the degrees of Bachelor of Sacred Theology and Master of Divinity. He was awarded honorary doctorates by Nashotah House and the University of the South at Sewanee. After the Korean War he became an Army Chaplain and served as rector of churches in Ohio and Florida, retiring from the Army Reserve with the rank of Colonel.

His tenure encompassed the difficult recession years of the eighties, but the diocese continued to grow. His wife of 54 years, the former JoAnne Nida Patterson of Winter Park, Florida, was one of his greatest supporters. She said, *"He thought it was more intimate to have small groups. He started with Bible study. This drew people in because they got to know each other. It was a very beautiful thing to see."*

Consecrated Bishop of Dallas in 1983, he started 14 new parishes including Christ Church, Plano, one of the largest congregations in the national church. In Texas he served on the Board of Trustees of the Episcopal Theological Seminary of the Southwest in Austin, St. Mark's School of Texas, the Episcopal School of Dallas, and the Children's Medical Center of Dallas.

Bishop Patterson was forced to resign as Bishop of Dallas in 1992 due to ill health. He died in 2006 from leukemia in Florida at the age of 75.

JAMES MONTE STANTON - the Theological Bishop

JAMES MONTE STANTON began his ministry in the Church of Christ (Disciple). He was born in Atchison, Kansas, in 1946. He and his wife, the former Diane Hanson, have two children, Jennifer and Justin. He was graduated from Chapman College, Orange, California, and Lexington Theological Seminary in Lexington, Kentucky. He received the degree of Doctor of Ministry from Southern California School of Theology, Claremont, California. He also studied at the Church Divinity School of the Pacific, which awarded him an honorary doctorate, as did the University of the South and Nashotah House.

Converted to the Episcopal Church as an adult, he was ordained in 1977. From 1977 until 1981, he served as Vicar of St. Stephen's, Stockton, California; from 1982-87 he was Rector of St. Luke's, Cedar Falls, Iowa; then Rector of St. Mark's Glendale, California from 1987 until 1992 when he was elected 6th Bishop of Dallas. He served as a chaplain in the US Army Reserve, and is known for his work in the National Episcopal Cursillo Movement.

Bishop Stanton inherited a diocese torn by the arrival of a new Prayer Book and changes in the roles of women and homosexuals in the church, but for twenty years he has managed to hold together what has become one of the most diverse dioceses in Anglican Communion. He remained faithful to the church when many of his friends had departed, guiding a diocese where the parishes ranged from front-of-the-line liberal to ultra conservative. Few modern day clerics have ever faced such a challenge.

Yet he has declared that *"these have been the most challenging, fulfilling, and joyful years of my ministry."* Bishop Garrett would have been proud.

He will be remembered for his leadership in the Episcopal Church and in the broader Anglican Communion for defending "the faith once received," as a friend and supporter of many African bishops and dioceses, for strengthening the diaconal ministry in the diocese, and for leading the Diocese of Dallas through a strategic planning process that resulted in planting five suburban churches and eight other ethnic churches, including a church for homeless people. His episcopate also saw an influx of younger ordinands, the dispatch of bi-vocational priests to serve in rural areas, and the founding of Camp All Saints, the diocesan camp at Lake Texoma. The Diocese of Dallas grew under the leadership of Bishop Stanton, while the vast majority of dioceses of the Episcopal Church were in decline.

The announcement of Bishop Stanton's retirement at the end of May, 2014, was received with real regret. We are happy to dedicate this little history of the Cathedral Church of St. Matthew to him, in gratitude for his twenty-two years of devoted service.

"AN EXPRESSION OF THE KINGDOM OF HEAVEN"
SAINT MATTHEW'S FIRST CHURCH
AND LATER FIRST CATHEDRAL
ELM AND LAMAR STREETS
1870-1874

Illustration by David Farrell

CHAPTER FIVE
OUR FIRST VERY REVERENDS

Each of the nine Right Reverend Bishops just described was responsible for the overall supervision of his diocese, but each parish, including St. Matthew's, looked for leadership to its own rector, customarily called the Reverend. So how did the rector of St. Matthew's parish come to be called the VERY Reverend? Let's go back a bit.

The four-year Civil War had been a time of privation for Dallas, as elsewhere across the South. Most of the able-bodied male citizens joined the Army, and many never returned. There being no one to plant wheat, those left at home learned to like corn bread. Coffee, salt, and leather grew scarce and disappeared. Baled cotton was confiscated by the Confederate Army to serve as breastworks, leaving the civilian population almost naked for want of cloth. There was inflation. There was the sudden influx of slaves sent over the border from Louisiana to safety by their planter owners.

Then, in 1865, the Confederacy lost its bitter war. For almost a decade, U. S. Army tribunals replaced civil courts in Texas, while at the same time Freedmen's Bureaus attempted to find a place in society for the 200,000 Blacks cast adrift in Texas by the abolition of slavery. There was inevitable psychic damage. Texas came out of Reconstruction with a basic distrust of government.

Some stayed proud. A prominent street in today's Dallas honors HENRY S. ERVAY, who in March 1872 refused to resign his post as Mayor of Dallas as ordered by General J. J. REYNOLDS, military governor of Texas. Ervay chose jail rather than to desert his citizens. Later he was vindicated and returned to serve out his term, a Southern hero of Reconstruction days.

Small and weary as Dallas was, many newly freed slaves and ruined white plantation owners gathered here because the economic opportunities offered were marginally better than those available in other parts of the exhausted South. Still, Rector Rottenstein's return to his city at the close of the war presented him with an intimidating task. All of St. Matthew's parish records had perished in the Great Fire. His congregation was largely dispersed, leaving a total of six communicants, all women. He reinvigorated this dispirited and diminished congregation, but his strength had been spent. After his death in 1868, St. Matthew's sought a younger, more vigorous pastor.

God needed a champion. Dallas was boisterous, crowded, noisy, uncouth, disorderly, and full of strangers. Hundreds still made a living hunting bison. Herds of longhorn cattle being driven to Kansas City crossed the Trinity River practically at the town's doorstep. (You can see them immortalized in bronze on Young Street across from the Dallas City Hall.) One hundred professional gamblers made their homes here, easily supported by sixteen gambling houses, but there were only four churches (Church of Christ, Episcopal, Methodist, and Presbyterian). These were the years of gunfighters and robbers, pickpockets and burglars, drunks and con men. The KKK emerged, bringing its inevitable troubles. Hogs still rooted and wallowed in the muddy streets.

The growth of Dallas had been stunted not only by war but also by its lack of commercial water transportation. The only alternative being ox cartage, a slow and cumbersome business, many still hoped (against hope) that the Trinity River could be navigated if properly managed. In 1868 the *Sallie Haynes,* our last sad nautical venture, set sail. An anonymous poet urged her on.

Holy Heritage

> *Some people say it is all stuff.*
> *It never will reach Porter's Bluff.*
> *But if the captain don't run out of means*
> *He'll land her safe in New Orleans.*

The *Sallie Haynes* ended up hopelessly stranded forty miles down river, and by the eighteen seventies our would-be port city was forced to turn to railroads. The Houston and Texas Central received 115 acres of land (including right-of-way that is now Central Expressway), plus $5,000 cash, to lay its tracks through Dallas. In a few years, a crowd of 4,000 cheering people would welcome our first locomotive. It was to have a special significance for Episcopalians.

A new era was dawning. The Episcopal Church had put down its ancient roots. Bishops had been planted, and with them, on the horizon, the deans of the coming cathedral. Who were they? Each of these devoted men, having a title in common (they were all Deans of St. Matthew's Cathedral), brought a unique personality to our hallowed space. They made our history. Where did they come from?

Everywhere! It was not until the twenty-first century that a native Texan was elected Dean of St. Matthew's. Some of these "foreign" deans seem to have regarded Dallas as a stepping stone along a career path rather than a destination. Eleven moved on after five years or less. Five served from seven to ten years. Only three have remained for more than ten years. Did they see Dallas as a mission field? Did they realize, especially in the early days, that they would be serving a congregation which thought of themselves as Texans first, Confederates second, and only third as citizens of the US of A? Did they, like the Spanish Franciscans before them, seek to civilize as well as convert?

In all the ways that matter, Dallas and its citizens after the Civil War were much like Dallas and its citizens today. How could we, a bunch of ordinary Texans, become the Mother Church of a diocese? Remember what Bishop Garrett called us to be? *"Here, as at the central heart, must the warm glow of spiritual life be maintained, and the sweet harmony of an able ministry, a beautiful ritual, and profound purity be found."* Harmonious? Beautiful? Profound? Does that sound like us? Bishop Garrett set the bar high.

Who were the men who were brave enough to take us on? Meet those who have borne the honor of being addressed as the Very Reverends.

SILAS DEANE DAVENPORT - 2nd RECTOR (1868-74), 1st Dean (1874-1877)

In October of 1868 Bishop Gregg approved the transfer of the Rev. SILAS DEANE DAVENPORT to Dallas from Marshall. His choice was inspired. During a visit a year later the Bishop awarded $100 to St. Matthew's, stating that Davenport *"had won the confidence and affection of the people."* Shortly thereafter a small rectory was built for him by the young men of the parish, a tribute to his service by a grateful community.

Davenport was born on July 21, 1829, on his father's farm in Columbia, Tyrrell County, North Carolina. He was named for SILAS DEANE, a controversial figure during the American Revolution who had been a member of the Continental Congress, and as their representative in France had recruited Lafayette to the American cause. Ordained deacon (1856) and priest (1859) by THOMAS ATKINSON, Bishop of North Carolina, Davenport was called to the mission field in Texas, where he served in Corpus Christi and Waco, and like Rottenstein as a Chaplain in the Confederate Army during the Civil War. He married his first wife, LOUISA GORDON ARMISTEAD, a cousin of Confederate General LEWIS ARMISTEAD, in 1864 in Waco. They had one daughter, born in 1868. Tragically, Louisa died soon after the baby's birth.

When the new Rector arrived in Dallas, he was a young widower who at first lived with his little daughter in the same down-town Keaton hotel which had housed his predecessor. Episcopal services were still held in the County Court House, but Davenport soon became aware of his parishioners' deep longing for a church building of their own. First moving St. Matthew's to a blacksmith's shop at Austin and Market Streets for the rent of $12 month, he used the Bishop's $100 to purchase a lot on Elm and Lamar Streets for the erection of Dallas' first Episcopal building. Financially, things were looking up.

JOHN WILLIAM ROGERS, in his *Lusty Texans of Dallas,* described some of the experiences, bad and good, which Parson Davenport had to deal with after his arrival in Dallas. (The title of Parson, meaning the Rector of a parish, was in general use in England at this time.) According to Rogers, Davenport was wounded twice by gunfire for his criticism of primitive behavior on the part of Dallasites. (A cowboy had ridden his horse around the church during services, shooting out all the windows.) These were the lawless post-Confederate years of the Younger-James gang and Belle Starr. The civilized streets of North Carolina must have seemed very far away.

On the other hand, KATE KEATON, the little daughter of the hotel proprietor, remembered being interrupted one day during piano practice by a group of the town's leading gamblers requesting an interview with Parson Davenport. When he was summoned, he received a bag of coins and a presentation speech that went something like this: "*Parson, we heard that you were figuring on putting up a meeting house, and we figured, too, that you were having an up-hill pull, and as you have treated us like we were more or less human, we thought we'd help you out a little, so we passed the bag and want you to take it and buy lumber and start your meeting house.*"

Due in part to Davenport's Christian behavior and the gamblers' generosity, St. Matthew's first church building soon moved from dream to reality. Some parishioners felt that the chosen lot at Elm and Lamar was too far out of town to attract a congregation, but nevertheless ox carts set out to Jefferson in the Texas piney woods for lumber, a 380 mile round trip. In 1870, Bishop Gregg returned to Dallas to confirm ten people and to lead a procession from the old blacksmith home to the site of the future St. Matthew's, where he laid the cornerstone. Valued at $6,000, the new church boasted a pipe organ, given by a vestryman, and a choir of two sopranos, two basses, and one tenor. The organist was the 12-year old daughter of a communicant. Our pride and joy was an enormous bell, the GREAT MATTHEW, the tribute of a group of New York merchants. It was to remain a visual and aural symbol of Christian presence in the Metroplex. We ring it still.

Davenport's nine-year incumbency was an exciting time for Dallas, now beginning to show signs of adolescence. One admirer remarked, it *"was growing like an enchanted castle in a fairy tale."* The small community was becoming famous as a source of buffalo hides, and immigrants heading west paused here to take advantage of their last chance to take on supplies before they hit the western deserts. In 1873 the Houston and Texas Central Railroad was extended to Denison, where it connected with the mighty MKT Line which offered service to faraway St. Louis. The following year the Sanger Brothers opened their seminal store, as Dallas' future as a fashion center appeared on the horizon.

For St. Matthew's, there was greater to come. In 1874 ALEXANDER CHARLES GARRETT, first Bishop of Dallas, declared the little town on the Trinity his see city, and the frame building on Elm Street was transformed overnight from parish church to cathedral, spiritually equal, as Bishop Garrett announced, to Canterbury, York, Antioch, Rome, or Constantinople. Once a mere rector, Davenport assumed the title of dean.

Soon the newly promoted sanctuary became a focus of Dallas' musical heritage, boasting a choir proficient enough to be led by a Professor Bayer in a Christmas songfest, the first of many. All

Holy Heritage

the good voices in the community took part. The same year, a Professor Otten produced Dallas' first opera with a full orchestra, *Martha*, by Friederich Von Flotow, at Fields Theater. A Swiss glee club sang. A group of bell ringers rang. We even had our own band. Not bad for a town only a generation away from a huddle of tents.

By 1876 Dean Davenport proudly reported 127 communicants, and St. Matthew's first cathedral church, no longer large enough to house a growing congregation, was sold for $7,500 to make way for a larger building at Commerce and Kendall Streets. An attempt to move the original cathedral to the new site ended in collapse, but bits of it were later incorporated into the larger structure.

The next year Great Matthew rang out its joyful notes to celebrate the Rector's second marriage. His bride was the former MARTHA HELEN SCRUGGS and the couple was blessed the following year with the birth of a daughter, HELEN DEANE DAVENPORT.

But missionary work over eight counties by horseback or buckboard had exposed Dean Davenport to severe winter weather and in 1877 he died from its effects. At his funeral his Bishop remembered, "*He was always the gentleman, the Christian, and the clergyman. He never forgot the breeding of the first, the meekness of the second, or the dignity of the third.*" No mean accolade.

The *Times Herald* wrote that the Very Reverend Silas Deane Davenport "*entered into rest January 1, 1877, aged 47 years. Through all these anxious years his pure life, strict integrity, patient courage, and strong faith won the affectionate esteem of all classes of the community and conquered success. Twice a delegate to the General Convention from the Diocese of Dallas, he was wise in counsel, prudent in expression, faithful in duty, loyal in devotion, reliable in friendship, and strict in every relation in life. He was a man the Church can ill afford to lose, and whose place it will be very difficult to fill.*"

He was buried in Pioneer Cemetery, where his little daughter Helen soon joined him.

Mary Foster Hutchinson

2nd STEPHEN HERBERT GREEN, the High Church Dean (1877-1882)

A Second Cathedral

Six months after Davenport's death our second cathedral formally opened at Kendall (Field) and Commerce Streets, under the deanship of STEPHEN HERBERT GREEN. Here at last was a real Anglican church building. Graceful arches and soaring pillars proclaimed its English Gothic style, the chancel windows of leaded glass being a gift of the Sunday School children. No one knew that this "finest church in Dallas" was destined to be St. Matthew's home for only thirteen years.

The future Dean Green was born in 1849 in North Carolina, the son of William Mercer Green, later first Episcopal Bishop of Mississippi, and Rachel Green. He was educated at Berkeley Divinity School in New Haven, Connecticut, and was ordained priest in 1873. Stephen and his wife, Cornelia Matilda Casey of Connecticut, had a large family. His eldest daughter, Charlotte, was born in Dallas and christened in St. Matthew's. He also served in churches in Connecticut, Mississippi, Illinois, Missouri, Tennessee, Maine, and Alabama. He was a delegate to General Convention, and the author of *"Manual for Use at Holy Communion."*

He assumed leadership of a St. Matthew's which housed the only pipe organ in town, played by one Gustavus Gyrstenburgerm, a political refugee from Saxony and Dallas' only professional organist. At the new Dean's urgent request, a vested male choir in the English tradition was soon organized. Vestments were still a novelty in Texas, but in Anglican usage expressed the equality before God of all who take part in the drama of our redemption and focus attention on the altar, not the personality of the altar party.

Unfortunately, Wippell's Ecclesiastic Emporium was not just around the corner. The ladies of the church, however, were equal

Holy Heritage

...ge, and both cassock and surplice were produced by ...at home, using an existing Mother Hubbard pattern, greatly to the satisfaction of Dean Green. He was, after all, a bishop's son and knew how things should be done in a traditional Anglican cathedral.

"THE CHRISTIAN FAITH IN STONE AND GLASS"
SAINT MATTHEW'S SECOND CATHEDRAL
KENDALL (FIELD) AND COMMERCE STREETS
1876-1893
Illustration by David Farrell

He kept up with the times. It was he who abolished the custom of supporting the parish by renting out the church pews. Voluntary contributions made by all were substituted, and seating became "first come, first served."

Dean Green's tenure was significant both for the parish and for the city. The Oxford Movement, reasserting Anglo-Catholic and high church theology and liturgy, was strong, and suited his sacramental feelings. Bishop Garrett lived nearby and was busy founding St. Mary's College. By 1879 a world famous tenor named Tagliapetri became the first noted artist to perform in Dallas, and in 1880 the Missouri, Kansas and Texas railroad (later affectionately known as the Katy) arrived. By 1881, Dallas had a population of 10,385, a new-fangled gadget called a telephone, and an annual state fair. Electricity was not far behind. Cotton was king.

After five fruitful years, Dean Green answered a call to become rector of the Church of the Redeemer in Elgin, Il. His parishioners found him *"a man of great magnitude, esteemed and highly respected."* But for him, five southern years were enough. At retirement, he settled in White Plains, New York, and died in 1919 in Scarsdale.

The Rev. John Davis of Denison and the Rev. Richard Collison became temporary supply priests while St. Matthew's sought a new leader. They found him at home.

3rd JOHN DAVIS, the Erudite Dean (1882 - 1884)

JOHN DAVIS was the first of Dallas' intellectually gifted deans. He was born in Abbeville, South Carolina, in 1851, and was educated at Furman University, the University of the South, Sewanee, Tennessee, and Nashotah House in Wisconsin, where he received a Doctoral degree in Theology. In 1883 he married Tully Murphy. They had one child, Eleanor. He served in various churches in Texas and Missouri before coming to St. Matthew's from St. Luke's Church, Denison.

Dean Davis' Dallas had a population of over ten thousand,

mostly Anglo, German, and French, and continued its position as a music center. A 1,200-seat opera house was built, where a cheering crowd celebrated Dallas' first production of the *Mikado*. The city was served by 20 churches and 300 saloons. It boasted a baseball team and a city hospital. Sanger Brothers store, always in the technological vanguard, daringly installed three electric lights to focus the attention of customers on their wares. Dallas was booming.

At St. Matthew's, faithful parishioners donated new pipes for the organ, and built a substantial and beautiful iron fence around the property. There was a marked increase in the number of baptisms and confirmations. Twenty acres were acquired by the diocese as a site for the future St. Mary's College. But Bishop Garrett was not pleased. The total number of communicants was not growing, partly due to a shifting population, and, in the Bishop's opinion, a shifting clergy. In his 1884 Annual Report the Bishop complained that *"a deep sleep had fallen"* over the Dallas church, which had *"lost all its pride,"* and succumbed to *"the busy tongue of gossip."*

That same year Dean Davis left Dallas to become Dean of Trinity Cathedral, Little Rock, Arkansas. Was there some connection between Garrett's dissatisfaction with St. Matthew's and Davis' departure? Or perhaps Dean Davis felt the need for a more challenging climate. In 1895 he answered a call to the mission field to serve in Tokyo, Japan, where he founded the Chair of Ecclesiastical History in St. Paul's Theological Seminary. Becoming proficient in his adopted language, he wrote *"Chapters in Church History"* in Japanese.

Returning to the United States, he served churches in Indiana before retiring to Hannibal, Missouri. There he developed a third profession, and as a botanist of distinction contributed plants and research to Harvard University's famous Arnold Arboretum. He died in his birthplace, Abbeville, South Carolina, in 1924 at the age of seventy.

4th WILLIAM MUNFORD, the Soldier Dean (1884 - 1888)

William Munford was St. Matthew's military dean. He was born on August 16, 1829, in Isle of Wight, Virginia, and educated at the College of William and Mary. Appointed Lt. Colonel in the 17th Regiment of the Virginia Infantry, he was a member of the staff of General James Longstreet, second in command to General Robert E. Lee, during the Civil War.

After Lee's surrender, Munford served churches in several states, including Alabama, Virginia, Louisiana, Tennessee, and Maryland. In 1880 he was rector of St. Paul's Church, Columbia, Mississippi. He and his wife, the former Frances Ball, had five children.

In Dallas he found a city growing up in the world of journalism. A. H. Belo had moved his Galveston newspaper to Dallas, absorbing the existing *Dallas Herald*, and the *Dallas Morning News* was born. Our city now housed 30,000 people, enough to attract the touring Lily Langtry, most inspiring actress of the day and later mistress of King Edward VII. We also cheered an annual comic opera in the park, and supported a public zoo.

Religion was not lagging behind. By 1888, Dallas boasted 34 churches and was the scene of major revivalist activities. At first, St. Matthew's grew and flourished as Dean Munford introduced the popular custom of holding a three-hour service on Good Friday. But there were rumblings in the Second Cathedral, and they were not theological. When this noble brick edifice had been erected, little attention had been paid to plans to run a railroad through the adjacent lot. But over time, as railroad service grew, the hooting of horns and the crash of machinery rose to a pitch that drowned out the human voice. A frustrated congregation was eventually forced to acknowledge that their situation was untenable. The railroad could not be re-routed. St. Matthew's would have to move.

Perhaps if the *Sallie Haynes* had not run aground, river traffic could have been established and the railroads could have taken their clamor elsewhere. But the railroad builders held Dallas' future in their hands. Reluctantly Dean Munford led a search to find a new church location. It took longer than anyone expected and after four difficult years with a shrinking congregation, the Soldier Dean left Dallas for the Diocese of Easton in Maryland.

Lt. Colonel/Dean Munford died in 1904 in Richmond, Virginia, where he is buried in Hollywood Cemetery.

5th CHARLES WILLIAM TURNER, the English Dean (1889 - 1893)

After the departure of Dean Munford, the Rev. William Guion was supply priest at St. Matthew's until a new Dean was found. He was CHARLES WILLIAM TURNER, born in England in 1843 and an old friend of Bishop Garrett, who had been after him for years to come to Texas. Turner wasn't enthusiastic, but finally gave way to some rather strong arm-twisting, and accepted a call to become Dean of St. Matthew's in Dallas in 1889.

CHARLES WILLIAM TURNER was graduated from St. Mark's College, Chelsea, London, in 1864. He taught at the Normal School there in 1866 and was admitted to Deacon's Orders in 1867. Shortly thereafter, he and his wife, the former Ellen Elizabeth Reid, moved to Hawaii, where he served on the faculty of St. Alban's School, Honolulu. The couple emigrated to the US mainland in 1869, where he was employed as an assistant at Trinity Church, San Francisco. Both of the couple's daughters, Ethel and Edith, were born in California. He was ordained priest in 1870 and became Rector of St. Paul's, Oakland, California, and in 1874 Rector of St. John's Church, Long Island City, New York. From 1876 to 1889 he was rector of St. Matthew's Church, Brooklyn, NY. A son, John Lawrence, was born in New York.

The year of Dean Turner's arrival here, 1889, was a busy one for the Diocese as St. Mary's College opened with 24 students and Dallas grew to become the largest city in the state. But it soon became apparent that Dean Turner's sermons would not breach the sound barrier on a Sunday morning any more than Dean Munford's had. Consequently, attendance continued to shrink, and the handsome Cathedral on Commerce Street was soon swallowed up in debt and cacophony. Cathedral Number Two was never finished, paid for, or consecrated. No one was very surprised when it was vacated and sold to a Cable Car company for the robust sum of $60,000.

The Third Cathedral

During Dean Turner's tenure, a site for a new cathedral was purchased at the corner of Canton and Ervay Streets. On this site rose the greatest and most famous cathedral in St. Matthew's history. In 1893, with the adjoining lot purchased, Bishop Garrett laid the cornerstone for our third cathedral, using the cornerstone of the second.

St. Matthew's grandest cathedral would have been imposing in any setting. Its massive Gothic buttresses rose regally above a 170-feet long nave. Constructed of local limestone and oak, it was designed to accommodate a congregation of 900, 30 choristers, and six priests. Adjacent buildings housed a diocesan house seating 200, a gymnasium, reading and guild rooms for men and women, a kitchen, and coffee rooms. One of the largest in America at the time, this handsome cathedral attracted architects from all over America and came to be considered the most beautiful church in the State of Texas. It would be our home for almost forty years.

Our cathedral was not the only architectural achievement of the City of Dallas. In 1892, "Big Red," as Dallas County Courthouse was called, rose at a cost of $350,000 on Main Street, adorned with fabulous two-winged dragons called wyverns. In the world of commerce, Sanger Brothers changed American retail forever by abolishing bargaining and establishing fixed prices for its merchandise. In 1891 a Carnegie Library opened with 10,000 books. All this was especially admirable since in 1890 Dallas

"THE THIRD VISION AND ASPIRATION OF THE PEOPLE"
SAINT MATTHEW'S THIRD CATHEDRAL
CANTON AND ERVAY STREETS
1895-1927

Illustration by David Farrell

had suffered a major flood, and in 1893 a freezing winter which turned the Trinity River into a skating rink, while a financial panic overwhelmed America.

After applying for naturalization, Dean Turner left Dallas in 1893 just as our magnificent new cathedral was finished, and returned to New York to be Rector of St. John's Church, Huntington, Long Island. Toward the end of his life, he served at Grace Church, Menomie, Wisconsin, before retiring to Manhattan.

The father of our greatest church building died in New York City in 1920 at the age of 76, guided to his rest (may we hope) by choirs of gothic angels. Following funeral services at the Cathedral Church of St. John the Divine, he was buried, appropriately enough, in Kensico Cemetery, Valhalla, New York.

6th JAMES HUDSON STUCK, the Alaskan Dean (1894 - 1904)

Every institution has its celebrity. Hudson Stuck, first conqueror of North America's highest mountain, Mt. McKinley, is ours. He might not have relished the title. He described his elevation to the position of Archdeacon of the Yukon to a friend as his "glorious emancipation from Dallas." St. Matthew's was, for him, a middle rung in a very high ladder.

JAMES HUDSON STUCK was born in a London suburb in 1863 into a lower middle class family of stolid Presbyterians unable to pay for the education his academic brilliance deserved. Disinclined to embrace either his father's business or religion, he joined two other frustrated English youngsters and ran away from home, emigrating in 1885 to Texas on the flip of a coin. (Had the other side landed upward, the trio would have sought their fortunes in Australia.) Railroad magnates had assured the youths that good jobs awaited them in the Lone Star State. They found San Antonio full of deceived Englishmen and jobless.

Stuck took what he could get, a post as a hired hand at a ranch in Junction City, population 500, 120 miles west of Austin. He was

Holy Heritage

a city boy and not very good with horses, but was eventually hired to teach school in Copperas Cove (County Seat of Coryell County) for $40 a month. He was a good teacher, and soon moved to a better job in San Angelo, where he attended the local Episcopal Church and came to the attention of the Rt. Rev. JAMES STEPTOE JOHNSTON, Missionary Bishop of West Texas. Unexpectedly, the strange young Englishman declared his wish to study for the Episcopal priesthood.

How this happened is as mysterious as Stuck's first acquaintance with Anglicanism. The story of how God led Hudson Stuck to faith was something he kept to himself. But Bishop Johnston was badly in need of clergy and had at his disposal a scholarship to the University of the South in Sewanee, Tennessee. Stuck was offered the gift of an education and accepted. He devoured college like a starving man at a bakers' picnic, and in 1852 fulfilled his mentor's hopes by graduating from Sewanee with honors.

After he was made deacon and priested, he spent two frustrating years trying to run Grace Episcopal Church in Cuero, followed by a stop on the Chisholm Trail in South Texas. Neither job suited either priest or people. When offered the position of Dean of St. Matthew's Cathedral in the City of Dallas, he was quick to accept, taking up his new duties in 1894.

Dallas, with a population of 42,638, was still reeling from the Depression of 1893. Five banks had failed, and 5,000 people moved away. But Stuck was lucky. Economic recovery was quick, and by 1895, due largely to Dean Stuck's efforts, a $100,000 debt was paid off, and our magnificent cathedral was hallowed on the twenty-fifth anniversary of Bishop Garrett's consecration by no less a personage than the Presiding Bishop of the national church, with five other bishops assisting.

In 1899 the Cathedral parish celebrated its 25th anniversary and a daring Dallasite bought the city's first automobile. The turn of the century saw Paderewski and Sousa playing in Fair Park. Parkland Hospital was established. A golf course was built. The

Confederate Memorial was erected. The first movie house opened. Bachman's Lake was created. Dallas was on its way.

But none of this was quick enough for the new Dean. His methods, more governed by zeal than by discretion, attacked St. Matthew's and Dallas from a position of strength - his absolute assurance that he knew what was right and his inability or desire to compromise. Women were ordered in no uncertain terms to wear a particular kind of hat. Parishioners stalked out when he recited the Nicene Creed (complete with genuflection). He never faltered. He remained staunchly "high," insisting on *"presenting the great truth of Christianity in the unbroken historical claims of the church."* He initiated the popular celebration of a Midnight Mass on Christmas Eve. The congregation grew from 513 to 671 souls. He must have been a charismatic preacher.

Stuck was also a social reformer. At this time cotton mills in Dallas employed boys as young as ten who worked a twelve-hour day. While our most influential members, backed by *The Dallas Morning News,* supported this practice, the Dean, coming from a country which had already abolished child labor, worked tirelessly until the Texas Legislature revised the law. Were elderly women begging on the streets? He founded the Home for Aged Women. Were children hungry and untaught? He founded the St. Matthew's Home for Children. Were unmusical sounds emerging from the congregation and the choir? He insisted on a first rate boys' choir that *"the standard of music should be in keeping with cathedral churches the world over."* The boys rehearsed three times a week and were soon the outstanding choir in the city. Was the Diocese too absorbed in providing education for girls (a special mission of Bishop Garrett)? Stuck founded the St. Mattthew's Grammar School for boys.

Holy Heritage

The Call of the Wild

There was from time to time a disparity between the patient aims of Bishop Garrett and Stuck's "driving sense of haste," but all grieved when in 1904 Dean Stuck answered a plea from Bishop PETER TRIMBLE ROWE of Alaska, and became the Archdeacon of the Yukon. For years, traveling through the wilderness by dogsled, boat, and foot, he served his scattered wilderness flock, eventually being able to say that there was not a soul in Alaska who remained unbaptized. In 1914 his party of four amateurs, wearing moccasins with hand-made crampons strapped to the soles, became the first men to reach the summit of Mt. McKinley (which he preferred to call by its Indian name, Mt. Denali), a triumphant climax to a lifetime of hope and preparation. After scientific instruments showed that they had indeed reached the 20,000-foot plus crest of the highest peak on the continent, the little party - priest, postulant and lay - planted a cross, *"the sign of our redemption"* in the ice, and gathered around the newly christened top of North America to recite the *Te Deum*. For them, heaven and earth were indeed full of the majesty of God's glory.

The Archdeacon of the Yukon died on October 11, 1920, and is buried as he wished to be inside the Arctic Circle. Somewhere C. S. Lewis says that the Creator didn't make two blades of grass alike, let alone two saints. On that October day a feisty kind of saint entered into paradise from Alaska. James Hudson Stuck's glorious emancipation was complete.

Our most illustrious dean, Hudson Stuck has been honored along with John Muir with a feast day, April 22, on the liturgical calendar of the Episcopal Church.

HUDSON STUCK

CHAPTER SIX A
TRANSFORMING
HALF-CENTURY

If the deans of St. Matthew's Cathedral wished to civilize Dallas, they had a good measure of success. In the twentieth century the last living memories of the Confederacy died, the title of Texan became a sobriquet, and for the first time we all thought of ourselves as Americans. Before the century was over, the rustic had become the sophisticated.

The catalysts were growth and war.

The population explosion was in itself remarkable. The 1910 census lists Dallas as home to 92,104 citizens. By 1990 this number had risen to over a million. If areas we have come to know as the Metroplex are included, it approaches seven million today. And each and every one of us was and is an immigrant, from our Pleistocene predecessors for whom we stand proxy until now, adopted Texans because there is no other kind.

By the time Dallas was celebrating VJ Day, we were ready to grow up. But first the touching optimism of the Victorian era had to give way to the disillusionment of World War I and the reckless "flapper" age, the despair of the stock market crash, and great depression of the twenties and thirties. It was World War II that changed us. It homogenized America. There were no more cowboys and Indians, no more Yankees and Rebels. We are at last all citizens of the world.

Still, in-comers left their mark. Beginning in mid-twentieth century, waves of easterners moved into North Texas to meet the requirements of the dawning electronic age. Episcopalians of every stripe and accent found their way into our growing parish. St. Matthew's wasn't just a parochial backwater anymore. It was the cathedral church of an international city. Richard Salmon's dream of an Anglican colony in Texas had come true.

7th GEORGE EDWARD WALK, the Linguist Dean (1904 - 1906)

At the beginning of the century, however, Dallas still had a long way to go. When Dean Walk arrived in town, our mayor was still raising money by selling tickets to public hangings.

GEORGE EDWARD WALK was born in Kenton County, Kentucky, in 1857, the son of an Episcopal priest, the Reverend David Walk. He received B.A. and M.A. degrees from Bethany College in West Virginia, and attended Berkeley Divinity School in Middletown, Connecticut, where he excelled in church history and became proficient in Hebrew, Latin, and Greek. He began his career on the west coast, where he served as Rector of St. Andrew's Mission in Oakland, California, and went on to Trinity Church, San Francisco, where he was Rector for seven years, being responsible for the building of a magnificent, quarter-million-dollar church which became a lucky survivor of that city's 1906 earthquake.

Owing to the poor health of his wife, (although he was the one who would died young), Walk resigned from Trinity and became Rector of three churches in the mid-west, - first Good Shepherd

Holy Heritage

in Omaha, Nebraska, then St. Paul's in Council Bluffs, Idaho, and finally the Episcopal Church in Cedar Rapids, Idaho, from which he accepted an invitation to succeed Dean Stuck at St. Matthew's.

The Dallas Dean Walk met in 1904 was now the leading drug, book, jewelry, and wholesale liquor capital of the Southwest. It remained the center of trade in cotton, grain, and buffalo. It led the world in manufacturing saddlery and cotton gin machinery. Its up-to-date citizens rode from floor to floor at Sanger Bros. on a newfangled gadget called an escalator.

But commerce was not its only concern. During Dean Walk's tenure, land was purchased for Fair Park and his parishioners enjoyed the Metropolitan Opera for the first time (*Parsifal*, no less). The 25th anniversary of the annual German Saegerfest with the Chicago Symphony boasted a chorus of 1,000, and Sarah Bernhardt acted in a tent.

During his short term of office, Dean Walk increased the membership of St. Matthew's to 1,800 souls, and was responsible for building a rectory for himself and his successors. His many civic activities included membership in the Masons, Elks, and Knights Templar. He died in office in 1906 at St. Paul's Sanitarium of acute diffuse pancreatitis, but he left the parish in good health. Bishop Garrett presided at his funeral and interment at Oakland Cemetery, Dallas.

8th HARRY TUNIS MOORE. Dean and Bishop (1906 - 1917)

Walk's short term was followed by the long term of HARRY TUNIS MOORE, born in Delavin, Wisconsin, in 1874, to Tunis Moore and Hannah Rector Moore, and educated at Hobart College, Geneva, New York, and Western Seminary, Chicago. Moore began his professional life as a member of the faculty of the University of Illinois at Champagne, where he met and married the former Annette Irene Reeme of Chicago.

After having served in San Antonio and Maryland, he came to

Dallas in 1906 from the Diocese of Springfield, Illinois, as eighth Dean of Saint Matthew's Cathedral. Under the aegis of Bishop Garrett, the Diocese was flourishing. Soon after the dean's arrival, St. Mary's College acquired its unique chapel, the gift of the Belo family, which owned the *Dallas Morning News*. This graceful English Gothic gem, which we now occupy as our cathedral church, was hailed by newspapers as "the Christian Heart of the City," and left us all dreaming that it might be so.

During Dean Moore the First's tenure (a second Dean Moore would be chosen in 1941), Dallas survived a damaging flood and a meningitis epidemic. In the second year of his deanship, due in no small part to the arrival of the motor age and the founding of Neiman Marcus, a real estate venture was launched which would have a profound effect on St. Matthew's: the birth of Highland Park. By 1910 another community which would deeply influence the future of the cathedral was established by a group of Mexican nationals just east of the business district. Happily, the city of Dallas welcomed the Federal Reserve Bank, natural gas, and White Rock Lake.

An aging Bishop Garrett was by this time in need of an assistant, and in 1917 Moore was elected Bishop Coadjutor of Dallas, with the right of succession on the death of the incumbent. He became Bishop of Dallas in 1924, and died here in 1955. An account of his achievements as bishop can be found in Chapter Four.

9th JACKSON H. R. RAY, the Mad Dean of Dallas (1918 - 1923)

When Harry Tunis Moore was elected Bishop Coadjutor in 1917, a new Dean had to be selected. The choice fell on a Mississippian. JACKSON H. R. RAY was born in 1886 on his father's 800-acre cotton plantation, the son of Capt. Jackson Harvell Ray, one of General Robert E. Lee's officers in the Confederate Army of Northern Virginia. Jack Ray's mother was his father's fourth wife.

Holy Heritage

His much older half brothers and sisters seemed more like uncles and aunts than siblings.

He went off to college planning to follow in the footsteps of one of his elder brothers and become a doctor. Or maybe, as his father wished, a lawyer. He did well at his undergraduate college, a small Methodist school called Emory and Henry in Abingdon, Virginia. Having been accepted as a graduate student at Columbia University, he spent some time as a wide-eyed tourist in New York City, and wandered one day into the Episcopal Church of the Transfiguration at Fifth Avenue and 29th Street, where he was much impressed by the beauty and serenity of that tiny house of prayer. He did not know it, but he had met his destiny.

Ray was a talented writer, but still unsure of his professional future he decided to join a group of fellow students on a bicycle trip through England, Scotland, and Wales. As he visited cathedral after cathedral with increasing awe, he came more and more captured by the Theology of the Eye, the teaching of religion through visual art. By the time he returned to New York, he knew that his future lay in the church.

In 1908 he entered General Seminary, NYC, and in due time was ordained deacon and then priest at the Cathedral Church of St. John the Divine in New York City. His first job was as curate at Zion and St. Timothy's in Manhattan, where he developed a life-long devotion to the theater and those who worked in it. The first person he prepared for confirmation was a dancer named Fred Astaire.

When his curacy was ended, the Rt. Rev. GEORGE HERBERT KINSOLVING, Bishop of Texas, (father of Ray's seminary roommate), offered him a job in Bryan as rector of St. Andrew's Church and the Episcopal chaplaincy at A&M University. "*I loved the Texans, for they were warm and responsive and real individuals,*" he wrote later. "*The period in Bryan was one of the most enjoyable interludes of a very happy career.*" But when WWI broke out, his military heritage called him to resign his pastorship and volunteer as an army chaplain. A perforated appendix frustrated this ambition, and WWI ended before he was restored to health. Soon after the Armistice was signed he accepted a call to be Dean of St. Matthew's, and chaplain to Army Air Force recruits at Love Field.

He arrived in a city celebrating with a victory parade of 25,000 triumphant citizens. Dallas was just beginning its recovery from the war, during which 15,637 citizens had been registered for the draft and 8,000 had actually served in the armed forces. The population of almost 160,000 paid thirty-two cents a gallon for gasoline, and the auto was taking over transportation. But like many men of his generation, the new Dean had never learned to drive an automobile. However, *"walking in Texas was even then a lost art "* and the parish soon presented its new leader with a car. When Ray became affectionately known as "the Mad Dean of Dallas" because of his eccentric driving, he was quietly assigned a chauffeur.

St. Matthew's was larger than any parish Dean Ray had ever led, but he was an immediate success. He became a great favorite with our thirteen hundred plus communicants and indeed won the admiration of all Dallasites for his self-sacrificial hospital work during the Spanish Influenza epidemic of 1919. He took devoted care of the cadets at Love Field, where training fatalities were frequent. For them, he caused a special chapel to be constructed with a tabernacle containing the Reserved Sacrament, originally dedicated to the memory of Walter Keeling, killed in WWI, and later consecrated to the feast of All Souls. Candles burned there day and night for the departed and those in peril. At this altar daily Eucharists were celebrated, an innovation for Dallas. (The altar of All Souls became the chief feature of the third cathedral to be transferred when we moved in 1930 to St. Mary's and declared it our fourth cathedral. It still serves us.)

After the death of his father, Dr. Ray brought his mother and sister to live with him in Dallas as the city he served survived prohibition, the rebirth of the KKK, and all the usual trials of life. But by and large his years here were good, successful years, happy years during which he began a healing mission and Bible classes for men and women. His choir, under the leadership of Carl Wiseman, provided a backdrop of Brahms and Handel equal to the best. The number of communicants reached 1,368.

Dr. Ray, however, had never given up his dream of serving the Church of the Transfiguration in NYC. He had married his long time love, Mary Elmendorf Watson, in 1922 and brought her back to Dallas, but hearing that Transfiguration's rector would soon retire, he quietly applied for the post. In 1922 he bade a fond farewell to Dallas and in 1923 he became the third Rector of the church known world-wide as The Little Church around the Corner.

Famous as the church of actors and weddings, high church TLCATC sometimes performs as many as forty weddings a day. Since the first nuptials in 1850, over 100,000 matrimonial knots have been tied there. The bride at the first wedding performed there by Dr. Ray was Grace Cecile Hatch, a Dallas girl.

A lover of the beauty of holiness, Dean Ray was one of our most attractive Deans.

He died in 1963 in Fairfield, Connecticut.

10th ROBERT SCOTT CHALMERS, the Scottish Dean (1924 - 1929)

ROBERT SCOTT CHALMERS must have thought that he had entered a raw, new town when he arrived in Dallas to undertake his duties as Dean of the Cathedral in 1924. He was born to William Chalmers and Helen Millar in Forfar, Scotland, a village with records going back to the year 306 AD. Nearby in the bonnie county of Angus, stands Glamis Castle, where Macbeth murdered Duncan and ghosts still walk. Chalmers grew up about ten miles away from this storied castle, where the sinister Glamis

Monster was housed, and where Elizabeth Bowes-Lyon, mother of Queen Elizabeth II, was raised. Chalmers was born into a land of enchantment.

But the future dean did not grow up enchanted. Trained as an attorney, he made a life for himself and his wife and children in Edinburgh, but in 1908 abandoned this career and the fabled history of his native shore to immigrate to America. Arriving via the SS Columbia, he settled in Boston. His wife, the former Adela Cox, and their two children, William and Margaret, passengers on the SS California, landed at Ellis Island in 1909.

What followed must have been seminary training, for by 1914 he is listed on the staff of St. Paul's Church, Akron, Ohio, and from 1915-16 he was Rector of Trinity Church in Tiffin, then from 1918-24 Rector of St. Mark's. Toledo. The couples' second son, James, was born in Ohio.

During this period he wrote a well received book entitled *Pastoral Series of Church School Lessons.*

Then he came to St. Matthew's, where he was especially interested in social causes, and St. Matthew's Home for Children. During his tenure a deaconess, Sister Patricia of the Order of the Holy Nativity, conducted conferences on the spiritual life of women. As was the case almost everywhere, he endured the tragedies of his time - the first blows of the Great Depression, mass unemployment, the Dust Bowl. The city was at the height of the Jazz Era, enjoying a dizzy population increase of 64% in ten years, and sending mail by air to New York. Like any adolescent, it was working hard to live up to its growth.

But no matter how raw the City of Dallas may have seemed, Dean Chalmers' fears must have been abated when he first caught sight of his cathedral church. For this was Cathedral Three, grandly orthodox in its traditional beauty. However, a decision was about to be made that would change the fate of St. Matthew's forever. After 34 years, the vestry voted unexpectedly and perhaps *sub rosa* to abandon their noble building on Ervay Street. Did their dean participate in this catastrophic decision? We do not know. Various reasons were given, among them that a site was needed nearer to the members' homes.

For some years Dallas' moneyed gentry had been leaving their fashionable mansions in The Cedars for the suburbs, especially the areas known as the Park Cities and Lakewood. Today, these neighborhoods would not be considered very far from downtown Dallas, nor would the ride to Ervay Street on Sunday mornings be considered onerous, but perhaps in the flapper years of the Twenties they seemed unbearably far away. Maybe. When the parish moved, it was to a location even more remote from Highland Park. It is an interesting side note that this Dean and his family lived at one time at 3400 Drexel Drive, a Highland Park address.

Some have suggested that the reason was size. Would the 900-seat nave have been too small for the growing congregation? Even with a membership of over a thousand, it is hard to believe that more than 900 people tried to worship at one time at the Ervay Street location. Did we really need a larger church? Or a grander church? When the one we had was nationally famous for its architecture?

It has also been suggested that the elaborate building was discovered to be unsound or cracked by Dallas' notorious shifting soil. But when it was demolished years later, experienced workers recorded that they had seldom seen such admirable construction. If foundation problems had been revealed, surely they would have been mentioned.

A more compelling reason for the decision to relocate to the corner of Ross and Henderson might simply have been the love the vestry and congregation felt for the deceased Bishop Garrett. He had been a stellar fund raiser, but perhaps not such a great investor. Five years after his death his beloved St. Mary's College was six million dollars in debt. Whatever the reason, our vestry voted to take over this obligation, abandon our Third Cathedral, and adopt the former St. Mary's Chapel as a temporary home.

St. Mary's property had been transferred to the cathedral in 1927, and in 1929 Ross Avenue, "The Fifth Avenue of Dallas," became our new address. Space in Garrett Hall went to a boys school which eventually became St. Mark's School of Texas.

Was this move intended to be permanent? Maybe not. Someone certainly had lofty plans. Even as late as the nineteen forties when I first sang in St. Matthew's choir, the model of a tremendous Gothic cathedral adorned a table in the parish hall. If this elaborate structure had ever been built, it would not have blushed to stand beside the iconic National Cathedral in Washington, D.C. Several architect's drawings of this palace among churches still hang for your inspection in Garrett Hall.

If such a vision ever did inspire the move from what was after all quite a handsome stone Gothic cathedral on Ervay Street, it was soon trumped by history. Gothic cathedrals are not cheap. When the stock market crashed of 1929 and 1932, followed by the Great Depression, the plan for a mega cathedral crashed too.

Dean Chalmers left Dallas the year of the crash, after having attended the Second Annual Catholic Conference in Wisconsin, where he presented several papers which give us a clue to his catholic liturgical leanings. From Texas he settled on the East Coast, where he became a prominent figure in controversy over the sanctity of marriage. His son William became an Episcopal priest and taught privileged boys at posh South Kent School in Litchfield, Connecticut.

In 1935, while serving as Rector of Grace and St. Peter's Church in Baltimore, Maryland, Dr. Chalmers was invited to preach at weekday services at hallowed Trinity Church, Manhattan, former parish of George Washington. On April 12, as he was being escorted to the pulpit, he fell dead in the central aisle. He is buried in Baltimore.

Dallas during Dean Chalmers' time, like the rest of the country, was broken by the collapse of its financial structure. Money was an almost imaginary commodity and mass unemployment

Holy Heritage

...e land. In 1931, 18,500 Dallasites were out of work. ...stayed afloat. Among the encouraging things which ...e the arrival of the Highland Park Cafeteria, and the East Texas oil boom. There were also some less reassuring things such as our first major automobile accident (41 people died), and the flapper era with its shattering of traditional values.

Some time in the dusty and impecunious Thirties, we realized that St. Mary's Chapel would be our permanent home.

Or would it?

"SHAPED BY THE FORCES OF HISTORY"
SAINT MATTHEW'S FOURTH CATHEDRAL
ROSS AND HENDERSON STREETS
1929 -
Illustration by David Farrell

Mary Foster Hutchinson

11ᵗʰ GEORGE RODGERS WOOD, the Disquieted Dean (1932 - 1940)

Murder of a Cathedral

It is Friday, September 3, 1937. Workmen have arrived at the corner of Canton and Ervay Streets. The hammers and the saws come out. Down comes the lofty tower which rose so proudly in English Gothic splendor. Down comes the soaring roof, down come the aisles, the transepts, the sacristy. Down comes the baptistry, where the tramps and homeless have folded their ragged bodies and lawless gangs have nested. Wrecking engineers marvel at the elegant, hand-done construction and count themselves lucky to have seen it dismembered. The hand-hewn blocks of stone seem too fine to discard. Later they will be sold as souvenirs. Big shovels lift stone and oak and debris into waiting trucks. And last of all, carefully dug out, two cornerstones appear, the vessels of so many hopes so long ago. A glorious building disappears with only the ghosts of choristers and prelates to weep.

It left illustrious memories behind. The House of Bishops of the Episcopal Church once assembled here, led by our own Bishop Garrett from his throne as Presiding Bishop. Hudson Stuck prayed here. Bishop Harry Tunis Moore was consecrated here. But in 1937 this sacred place, on which St. Matthew's third cathedral had stood, was sold for a used car lot.

The Dean who witnessed this crime was GEORGE RODGERS WOOD, born on November 6, 1887, in St. Clair, Pennsylvania, to Ward W. Wood, a Welshman, and Martha Rodgers. Like his immigrant father, he became a school teacher. His draft registration issued just before World War II describes him as a resident of St. Clair, short, of medium build, with brown eyes and black hair. He remained a bachelor all his life.

He was graduated from Lafayette College, Easton, Pennsylvania, and General Theological Seminary in New York in 1920, where he

Holy Heritage

stayed on as a Fellow until 1925. He served with the Society of St. John the Evangelist in Cambridge, Massachusetts, and at the Church of the Advent in San Francisco. By the time he arrived in Dallas in 1932, our great cathedral had already been abandoned for three years. Its execution had already been decreed and was not his fault. St. Matthew's had already moved to St. Mary's Chapel, where it is today. The city he arrived at was in the depths of the Depression.

An article from the Denton Record Chronicle dated March 1938 reveals something of Dean Wood's interests during his tenure here. It describes an eight-day preaching mission he conducted at St. Barnabas Church. Some of the subjects covered were "*What Is Religion?*," "*The Church, What Is It?*," and "*The Content, Technique, and Goal of a Christian Life*." He was theologically unsettled. He must already have been contemplating his eventual change of denomination while still in Dallas, where he celebrated the service of Holy Communion each day and held personal appointments each evening.

By this time the desperate Twentieth Century with its wars and rumors of wars was in full swing. His eleven year tenure was a difficult one as the cathedral climbed out of the debt accumulated during the move to St. Mary's and the lean years of the Depression, but through his efforts by 1938 the parish was almost debt free, an admirable achievement for the time and place.

Times were hard, but Dallas continued to expand. The Triple Underpass was built, and prohibition repealed, Texas Instruments was born, Skillerns installed our first commercial air conditioner, and the growing city invented the nation's first convenience store. Local ladies showed off their summer frocks by attending outdoor operettas at the Band Shell in Fair Park. Alas, this tradition met its doom one sultry evening when a visiting soprano opened her mouth for her high note and swallowed a confused June bug instead. The Summer Musicals were never the same after they were moved indoors.

Even more important for our future, America discovered

Texas at the 1936 Centennial Exposition, celebrated by all from Franklin Roosevelt on down.

It was a time of transition, both national and personal, as I suppose all time is. For Dean Wood, it was a time to move on. When he left Dallas, with the United States on the brink of war, he left much more than Texas and Dallas and the Cathedral Church of St. Matthew behind him. His World War II draft registration card, dating from 1941, lists his occupation as a candidate for the Roman Catholic priesthood at St. Paul's Priory in Keyport, New Jersey. Whether this goal was ever reached is unknown. Perhaps not, but when he died in 1943 and was buried in his parents' grave at the Odd Fellows Cemetery, St. Clair, Schuylkill County, Pennsylvania, it was a Roman Mass which sang him to his rest.

12th GERALD GRATTAN MOORE, the Gentle Dean (1941 - 1959)

During one of the anniversaries of his eighteen years as dean, GERALD GRATTAN MOORE declared, *"They have been happy and busy years of ministry, and I thank God for the joy of serving in such a responsive parish..."* Yes indeed. People do respond to goodness and gentleness. That hasn't changed since Cabeza de Vaca wrote in the sixteenth century, *"To bring all these people to Christianity, they must be won by kindness, the only certain way."*

The lives of Gerald Grattan Moore and Bishop Garrett ran parallel in many ways. Both were Irish by heritage, both immigrants from Canada. Our twelfth dean was born in Shelbourne, Ontario, Canada, in 1887 to the Rev. Henry Moore and his wife Lizzie, members of an Irish family of clergymen only recently arrived in the new world. (His older sister Kathleen was born in Ireland.) He was very proud of his Irish heritage and of his relationship to Anna Leonowens, the heroine of "The King and I."

In 1911 the family immigrated to the U.S., where Moore was graduated from Northwestern University and Western Theological

Seminary in Evanston, Illinois, being ordained priest in 1913. He served churches in Illinois and was Dean of St. Luke's Pro Cathedral in Evanston when called to become acting rector of Christ Church Dallas in 1941 and shortly thereafter St. Matthew's 12th dean. By the end of his first year the remaining debt assumed by our move to Ross Avenue had been discharged.

During his long tenure this gracious pastor baptized 15,000 souls and married 1,000 couples. He was largely responsible for the construction of the Great Hall and activities center connecting the Cathedral and Garrett Hall, opened in 1955 on the parish's 98th birthday. It contained space for Christian education, meeting rooms, a gift shop, a library, and a counseling center.

Much of his deanship was challenged by World War II, a hazardous time for Dallas and all of America. Prisoners of war occupied barracks at White Rock Lake. Thirty thousand men and women in three continuous shifts were building tanks in Grand Prairie. In Dallas alone, 376,085 ration books were distributed. But in spite of all, by 1944 Dean Moore was able to raise $14,000 in war bonds.

Political turmoil largely quieted the beginnings of a different turmoil, a challenge of faith, which was even then beginning in the church. In 1944 in Hong Kong the first female Episcopal priest was quietly ordained. Other changes were coming. Through all this, Dean Moore remained serene.

Gerald Grattan Moore was dean when I first sang in the St. Matthew's choir under the direction of Henry Sanderson just after WWII. He heard my first confession and presided at my wedding. I felt his love, and that of his sweet sister, known to us as Miss Kathleen, who kept house for her bachelor brother all his adult life. He retired in 1959 and died in 1972 in Tulsa, Oklahoma. He is buried in Chicago, where he spent so much of his youth.

When many of us now known as the Greatest Generation gaze in memory at that unambiguous time, a gentle Dean Moore smiles back.

GREAT MATTHEW
"THE ANCIENT BELL AT HOME IN ITS COT"

GREAT MATTHEW

The 1,500 pound bell which calls us to worship was originally a gift to Bishop Garrett from the merchants of New York City, using metal from an older bell, which had hung from the tower of Bishop Gregg's 1872 church at Elm and Lamar Streets. The recast bell adorned the Commerce Street Cathedral for 12 years, and in 1893 was installed in our third and greatest cathedral on South Ervay. When that structure was demolished in 1937, Great Matthew, scorned and neglected, went into storage.

In 1945 Dean G. G. Moore was responsible for resurrecting our bell and, finding it too heavy to be housed in our tower, built it a home in a special bell cot (small house) on the grounds of the present cathedral. The original cornerstone of the Ervay Cathedral has been reset in the northeast corner of the cot. It rings us into service on Sundays. It peals happy wedding bells. It tolls for funerals. During World War II it rang every day at noon for peace. Its inscription reads **"Gloria in Excelsis Deo, et in Terra Pax, Bona Voluntas Hominibus."** (Glory to God in the Highest, and on Earth Peace, Good Will toward Men.)

It is perhaps the oldest relic still preserved from St. Matthew's storied past.

Take a minute, friends, to visit and read and touch history.

Mary Foster Hutchinson

13th FRANK LOCKE CARRUTHERS, a Transitional Dean (1959 - 1964)

FRANK LOCKE CARRUTHERS presided as dean at the dawn of the theological troubles which would eventually fragment the Episcopal Church. He was born in Chicago, Illinois, and educated at Northwestern University and Seabury-Western Theological Seminary, from which he received the degree of Doctor of Sacred Theology. He served as a trustee of the Cathedral of Saint John the Divine in NYC and was a member of the Board of Managers of Missions and Church Extension from 1942-51. He was an experienced parish priest when he came to Dallas after twenty years as Rector of St. George's Church in Newburgh, New York. While in New York he served as clerical deputy to the Episcopal General Convention.

Dean Carruthers was a fighter, an ardent hunter, fisher, and boatman who stirred up a theological hornet's nest when he argued that the National Council of Churches had no right to dictate political, faith, or moral standards.

Locally, the administrative and financial life of the cathedral were strengthened during Dean Carruthers' era. Ecclesiastically speaking, it was significant for the publication of a book called *"Honest To God"* by an English bishop, John Robinson, the first shot of a liberal attack which would shake the Church to the present day. In 1965 there were three and a half million Episcopalians in America, a slight increase over previous years, but the number of parishes in the national church had decreased when the automobile made it possible to build large suburban parishes.

Oblivious of the religious storm soon to come - the arrival of women priests, the recognition of open homosexuals in the priesthood and episcopacy, and revisions to the Book of Common Prayer - the city of Dallas remained a major technical center and the home of the largest wholesale market complex in the world.

Dean Carruthers resigned from St. Matthew's in 1964 for personal reasons, leaving a congregation of 1500, and retired to his summer home in West Park, New York. Legally separated from the Episcopal priesthood, he later returned to Dallas where he became an official of a life insurance company and died in 1970.

His widow, the former Joan Buckley, died in 2011 in Dallas.

THE BLESSED SACRAMENT WINDOW

CHAPTER SEVEN
STAINED GLASS

Benjamin Franklin declared that nothing in this life is certain except death and taxes. He left something out. Change is also inevitable, no more so than in language. When I was first a communicant of the Episcopal Church, we often heard a confusing collect which began, *"Prevent us, O Lord, in all our doings."* The verb *"to prevent"* (which originally meant *"to go before"*) had come to mean *"to oppose."* Did the church really want God to oppose all our doings? Of course not. Obviously something had to be done.

It was done, as we shall see, in the Prayer Book revision of 1979, with the help of a St. Matthew's dean, Charles Preston Wiles. And because people were in the mood for change, a lot of other alterations took place, in tradition, in the Prayer Book and the Hymnal, and even in theology.

Some of the vivid color which defined our tradition got washed away. Oddly enough, when stained glass loses its color, it doesn't become easier to see through, but less so, for it is the color which carries the message of our redemption. In the era we will now describe, some hues became more vivid, some (hopefully of inferior worth) were discarded, some, sadly faded, returned to their former glory, and some were stored forgotten under the stairs.

We were all forced to acknowledge that, although God is indestructible, ecclesiastically speaking we live in a glass house. In the last quadrant of the Twentieth Century the house called

Anglicanism faced many challenges to its traditions of liturgy, teaching, and moral code. In this chapter we will follow the careers of five deans who faced these challenges and sought, according to their several convictions, to preserve the House of God.

14th CHARLES PRESTON WILES,
the Naval Dean (1964 - 1987)

The Almighty sometimes has dramatic ways of getting the attention of men He has selected to serve Him. St. Paul was struck blind on the road to Damascus. CHARLES PRESTON WILES fell off a submarine. It was not, of course, submerged at the time, only patrolling the Atlantic coast during WWII, but he emerged from the ordeal a changed man.

Born in New Market, Maryland, in 1918, and graduated from Washington College in 1939, he had been a perfectly happy teacher and school superintendent on his beloved Tangier Island in Chesapeake Bay before enlisting in the Coast Guard. After the typical cork-screw pitching of a surfaced submarine in rough weather ended his military career and necessitated a long convalescence at Bethesda Naval Hospital, he entered Virginia Seminary and was ordained to the priesthood in 1948. M.A. and Ph.D. degrees in Theology from Duke University followed, with specialization in church history and ethics.

In 1951 he married Mary McCallum, daughter of the Rector of St. Paul's Church, K. Street, Washington, D.C., where he was an assistant. He served his first parish as rector of St. Mary's, Burlington, New Jersey, for thirteen years, while also lecturing at the Philadelphia Divinity School. He was facing a church in turmoil.

Tradition and more progressive ways of being in the Episcopal Church were in tension. Bishop James Pike was being accused of heresy in California. The number of Episcopalians in the USA, after two centuries of growth, had begun to decline. Children failed to follow in the footsteps of their Episcopal parents, and many parents, as they saw their inherited traditions depart, departed with them. Since the Thirties, almost half of all Episcopalians had been converts from other churches. Three fourths of all Episcopal priests had been raised in other denominations. Tradition and ritual continuity fought with the new importance of a personal relationship with God as the determining mark of Christian discipleship.

The Book of Common Prayer was also under review. As Co-Chair of the Prayer Book Committee of General Convention, Dean Wiles helped to accomplish the dual tasks of making the service more accessible through the use of modern English and returning to the ancient catholic liturgies that restored the primacy of the Eucharist as the central act of worship. The Gloria regained its ancient place at the beginning of the service. Tenebrae and the Way of the Cross were revived. The peace was passed. The priest now faced the congregation from behind the altar.

But helping to create the Prayer Book of 1979 was not Dean Wiles' only accomplishment. On the home front, Garrett Hall became the location of the Anglican School of Theology, now the Stanton Center for Ministry Formation. An organ fund was set up and a living center for the elderly. Always interested in outreach to the young, Dean Wiles was instrumental in creating five Canterbury Houses on five area college campuses, led by five full-time chaplains.

During his tenure, new life arrived at St. Matthew's as four hundred Spanish-speaking parishioners were received by the bishop in one day. The city of Dallas also continued to expand with the birth of Southwest Airlines and Half Price Books. All three thrived. Today a vigorous Spanish-speaking ministry often draws more worshipers on Sunday morning than the English-speaking service.

Dean Wiles understood the Theology of the Eye, the capacity of visual aspects, such as stained glass, architecture, carvings, paintings, and vestments, for teaching Christianity. Beginning in 1966 he made many repairs and improvements to the cathedral fabric and established an endowment fund which grew to $700,000 to finance the dream of a new mega cathedral, a prospect still alive in the hopes of many. But if he had left no other legacy to his successors, he would live in our memories for his gift of the Christian Faith told through stained glass. In our weekly lives of worship and prayer, nothing outshines these portals. *Windows of Faith*, Dean Wiles' handsome book describing this mesmerizing glass, illustrates his triumphant fenestration of our space, finally achieved in the Nineteen Seventies.

After retirement from the cathedral, he served St. Luke's parish for several years as assisting priest. He died in Dallas in 2011 at the age of 93.

COME! MAKE A PILGRIMAGE!

In the Middle Ages, stained glass transformed cathedrals into galleries of glory, but it did more than that. It taught. When most Christians could not read or write, these windows were their university. Come, make a pilgrimage, follow their footsteps. Come quietly. Let the walls speak. Come when the sun is bright and interior lights are dimmed.

Stand before the high altar and look ahead of you, to the east. These are the original windows, completed in 1908 for St. Mary's College.. They depict women in the Church: Saint Mary the Virgin, Agnes, Ursula, Mary of Bethany, and Martha. On the left, the Three Kings deposit their gifts.

Now turn north. Just beyond the All Souls altar is the first of the Willet windows, showing the Twelve Disciples receiving the Blessed Sacrament. Turn left and on your right see a series of smaller windows dedicated to the Lesser Sacraments. You are now facing the little nook once used as a baptistry. Its windows depict the Baptism of Our Lord and His instructions to us to win the world.

Next turn left again, toward the present Baptismal Font, and then west. On our right hand are twin windows depicting God the Creator and the Fall of Man. Farther on, Jesus descends from the cross. We are now approaching the fabulous Resurrection Window, opposite the High Altar, supported by the four Gospel Makers. A left turn takes us to the Pentecost window, showing the disciples speaking in tongues.

A little detour to the right now brings us into the Narthex.. Here the clergy windows honor former deans. Reentering the church, we find on our right fenestrae lauding Alexander Charles Garrett, first bishop of Dallas.

As we continue east, we salute Anglican saints. Ahead and to our right on the south wall blazes the magnificent St. Matthew window, dedicated to our patron saint, twin to the Resurrection Window on the wall opposite. Now look up. The Stations of the Cross are high above us piercing the clerestory, bidding our souls take wing. A living Bible, our cathedral has preached its sermon.

15th ERNEST EDWARD HUNT III, the International Dean (1988 - 1992)

Dean Wiles used windows to make St. Matthew's adherence to the ancient theology of the church transparent. For Dean Hunt, things weren't quite so clear. *"Theology"* he thought *"comes from contact with culture."* The trouble is, culture changes. Should theology change with it? Is truth really the daughter of time?

ERNEST EDWARD HUNT III found his Christian faith in the halls of academia at Stanford University in California, where he was a history major. There the study of T. S. Eliot and W. H. Auden among other influences led to his baptism and confirmation in the Episcopal Church and determination to enter the priesthood. He received his seminary training at the Episcopal Seminary of the Southwest in Austin, from which he graduated with honors. During his stay in Austin a visit to a Mexican village awakened his interest in the mission field.

Hunt was of Welsh extraction, born in 1934 in Alamedo, California, and partially raised by a deaf grandmother whose freshly baked scones remained a happy memory of his childhood. In 1958 he married Elsie Maryan Beard and the following year was ordained in Grace Cathedral, San Francisco. He served in Salinas, California, St. Louis, and at the Church of the Epiphany in New York City, from which he came to St. Matthew's in 1988.

Here he planned to *"renew the Cathedral to act for the common good of the Diocese of Dallas, the parish, and the community, and preside over new growth of the Cathedral family."* This was no feeble goal. During his tenure, the national church continued to be divided along theological lines, and was marked by the consecration of the first female bishop. Culture, it seemed, for better or for worse, was altering dogma. Suddenly, or so it seemed to the average parishioner, each communicant was called upon to make personal theological decisions once left to the clergy.

Hunt's Dallas was a growing city of almost a million

inhabitants, an attractive place to live in, clean and smokeless because of the use of natural gas. It had developed a reputation as a moral city, church-going and respectable, a living example of Hunt's belief that history has an ultimate moral purpose. A natural student, Hunt, during his four years as dean, continued to earn degrees, an M.A. in Hispanic Studies from Stanford, and the Doctor of Ministry from Princeton Theological Seminary. He also served as a fellow at the College of Preachers in Washington, D.C. and of the Seminary of the Southwest.

His interests did not stop at Atlantic shores. He was on the Board of the Order of St. John of Jerusalem, which supported mobile ambulance care and an eye hospital in Jerusalem as well as clinics on the West Bank. He left St. Matthew's in 1992 to become Dean of the (American) Cathedral of the Holy Trinity in Paris, where he served until 2003.

Dean Hunt is the author of a book on the art of preaching and several novels. Now retired, he makes his home in Dallas.

16th PHILIP MENZIE DUNCAN II, the Floridian Dean (1992 - 2001)

PHILIP MENZIE DUNCAN II was the second St. Matthew's dean to go on to become a bishop. (See Chapter 4.) He left us in 2001 to be consecrated the Bishop of the Central Gulf Coast, an area including parts of Alabama and Florida.

Duncan was born in 1944 in Glen Cove, NY, receiving his B.A. from Baldwin-Wallace College in Berea, Ohio, his Master of Divinity from General Theological Seminary in NYC, and a Doctor of Ministry from Virginia Theological Seminary in Alexandria, Va. General Theological Seminary, The University of the South, and Virginia Theological Seminaries subsequently awarded him Doctor of Divinity degrees. He was married in 1970 to Kathlyn Anne Cowie. The couple has two sons, Andrew and Ian.

He served as Associate Rector of Christ Church, Ridgewood,

New Jersey, from 1970-72 and was rector of St. John's Church, Clearwater, Florida, a flourishing low church parish with 1200 members, from 1972 until his call to St. Matthew's in 1992. In Florida he was involved in many community and ecumenical affairs and was host of a TV show, "Sea of Faith."

Traditional religious leaders of his time did not swim in calm waters. Here in Dallas in the Eighties and Nineties, the neighborhood surrounding St. Matthew's was in demographic flux. The Spanish-speaking congregation thrived as the English-speaking congregation continued to shrink. Our Cathedral was well known - indeed in October 1998 its magnificent interior starred in an episode of the hit TV series, Chuck Norris' "Walker Texas Ranger." But fewer Texans were regular church goers.

At the same time, nationwide, a significant shift in American moral values was taking place. Almost half of all marriages ended in divorce, with a concurrent sharp rise in non-marital cohabitation and the birth of illegitimate children. Homosexuality was becoming an open way of life. On the political front, undeclared wars raged in Bosnia and Iraq, while terrorism raised its alarming head on every continent. Behavior was changing. We were changing.

Duncan faced a church racially and culturally diverse, composed of old and new members, professionals and day laborers, young and elderly, with traditional and modern ideas. He was well prepared to serve this salad bowl of opinion. Outreach was the game of the time. Dean and parish worked together in food pantries and ecumenical training programs. The Bishop's Camp, an outreach ministry initiated by Bishop Stanton and implemented by Deacon Diana Luck, was inaugurated, developing into one of the most significant outreach ministries in twenty years. Summer in the City brought youth groups from in and out of state together to pursue urban ministry. Social ministry, it seemed, trumped innovative theology.

Duncan became a deputy to General Convention, and served on the Boards of the Children's Foundation of the Diocese of

Holy Heritage

Dallas and the East Dallas Community Organization. He was a supporter of Thanks-Giving Square, and a member of the General Board of Examining Chaplains for the Episcopal Church. He was also an associate of the Society of St. John the Evangelist, and a member of the Order of St. John of Jerusalem.

His Texas success was not lost on his many admirers in Florida. In 2001, remembering his fruitful twenty years in the Sunshine State, they called him back to become Bishop of the Central Gulf Coast, one of the most beautiful areas in America, where he now makes his home in Pensacola.

17th MICHAEL SHANE MILLS, the Alabaman Dean (2002 - 2005)

Dean Mills faced a tough assignment. Episcopalians were in the midst of restructuring. None of us had ever expected to have to choose between schism and heresy, but many parishioners, nationwide, fearing that they would be obliged to accept innovations they could not countenance, were jumping ship. Was this the St. Matthew's that George Rottenstein and Alexander Garrett had sacrificed so much to hand down to us? Dallas was still growing but attendance at Saint Matthew's was down one third.

Things which the faithful had been taught ought not to be done were being done, while things which they had been taught ought to be done lay neglected. An openly practicing homosexual was installed as Bishop of New Hampshire. Significant numbers were leaving to join one of the so-called continuing churches, which sought to preserve traditional ways, or other denominations, in some cases abandoning organized religion altogether. For a while, Dean Mills was one of them.

MICHAEL SHANE MILLS was born in 1968 in Demopolis, Alabama, to Robert Eugene Mills and Carol Calloway, and received his Bachelor's and Master's degrees in English from the University of Montavello in his home state. After study at Nashotah House, he was ordained deacon in 1994 and priest in 1996. He was married in 1987 to the former Susan Lee. The couple has two children, Clare and John.

Before coming to St. Matthew's he served as Curate for Youth, Singles, and Young Marrieds and Curate for Christian Education at the Church of the Incarnation in Dallas, and later at Holy Trinity Church, Pelton, Durham County, England, in the shadow of magnificent Durham Cathedral.

Our city was emerging slowly from yet another recession, a dip in the economic roller coaster of the Eighties and Nineties which had seen ups and downs, and wild expansion both vertical and horizontal, laced with paralysis. During Dean Mills' tenure high rise building thrust skyward again, and Dallas could soon boast Victory Park, Uptown, and the Arts District, with their exuberant architecture. In 2004 the whole city united to help rescue almost 200,000 refugees from Hurricane Katrina. People began to refer again to Big D.

Although Dean Mills established the successful "Godly Play" curriculum in Sunday School, organized religion in general was not doing so well. At St. Matthew's, three large stained glass windows from our third cathedral were rescued and placed in the Foyer of our Great Hall, but nothing seemed to restore the spiritual peace of the church where they once hung. In 2005 Dean Mills joined those who felt that conscience led them elsewhere and left Anglicanism to be received into the Roman Catholic Church. He returned to his home state, but after receiving the Juris Doctor degree from the University of Alabama, Tuscaloosa, moved back to Dallas, where he briefly practiced law.

On October 1, 2011, he was restored to the Episcopal Priesthood. After serving churches in East Texas, he is currently Rector of the Church of the Good Shepherd in Dallas.

18th KEVIN EUGENE MARTIN, the Valiant Dean (2006 - 2012)

When Kevin Martin became our dean in 2006, the Episcopal Church seemed to be foundering. It must have taken a lot of courage to jump on board what looked like a sinking ship.

KEVIN EUGENE MARTIN was born in Cleveland, Ohio, in 1946, the son of Glen Eugene Martin and Clarissa Pauline Lambert Martin. He was graduated from Lewisville High School in Lewisville, Texas, in 1964. In that same year he married Sharon Smith at St. David's Church in Denton, Texas. During his undergraduate career at North Texas State University in Denton, he became one of the many spiritual children of the Rev. Emmet Waits, the luminous rector of St. Barnabas Church, from whom he received the vision of the "one, holy, catholic, and apostolic church' which Bishop Garrett had brought to Texas from the Oxford Movement.

Martin was graduated from NTSU in 1968, with a B.A. in history, going on to earn an M.A. in Theology from Berkeley Episcopal Divinity School in New Haven, Connecticut, with the highest honors. He was ordained deacon and priest in 1971. He served as curate at St. Matthew's Church, Wilton, Connecticut, and as rector of St. Matthew's Westville, Ohio, St. Luke's, Seattle, Washington, and Emanuel in Stanford, Connecticut. He returned to the Metroplex as Assistant Priest at Christ Church, Plano while serving as a consultant and speaker in congregational development on a full-time basis.

Martin was well-known as a preacher, teacher, author, and consultant throughout the Episcopal Church. He led a popular Leadership Training Institute in Evergreen, Colorado, was Executive Director of Vital Church Ministries, and for nine years served as Canon for Congregational Development in the Diocese of Texas.

In 2005, Martin became the acting dean of St. Matthew's

Cathedral, and on Easter Sunday, 2006, our 18th dean. During his first year, with the National Church in trouble, he led a congregation of 500 in raising 1.9 million dollars, partially to cover the over-due liquidation of the St. Mary's Estate debt. The remainder began restoration of Garrett Hall and bolstered youth programs, the parish food pantry, and the Pre-General Education Development (GED) program which became the Aberg Center. During his tenure Mi Escuelita (a Head Start preschool), the Bishop's Camp, and Summer in the City flourished.

Obviously, Martin brought great strength and stability to the Cathedral on the ground level. In the face of the turmoil in the Episcopal Church during his tenure, many people were leaving Episcopal churches. Was C. S. Lewis right when he declared that heresy, however deplorable, is less destructive than schism? Martin acknowledged the troubles of the devout as they were forced to decide whether to climb into a lifeboat and row away, or cling to the mast and pray for a fair wind.

"Both heresy and schism present themselves as the real Anglicanism." he declared. How, then, is the average parishioner in the pew to tell the difference? "Both the progressives and the conservatives," he warned, "have sold their church's birthright for the potage of immediate gratification." Maybe that's part of the trouble. His advice? Be patient. Our duty now is to remain gathered around our bishop and dedicated to the basic (if uncomfortable) truth that "we are all sent to be Christ in the world—" St. Matthew's as our ship of state, and heaven our destination.

Amen to that.

Dean Martin retired in 2012. He and his wife now make their home in Georgetown, Texas.

19th NEAL OTIS MICHELL, the First Native Born Texan and Current Dean (2013 - Present)

The first Texas-born Dean of the Cathedral, NEAL OTIS MICHELL came to St. Matthew's Cathedral after having served for twelve years on the staff of Bishop James Stanton, first as Canon for Strategic Development and then as Canon to the Ordinary.

Michell was born in Dallas, Texas, at Methodist Hospital, on February 16, 1953. He came into the Episcopal Church as part of the post-World War II boom, as part of a new church plant, St. Barnabas Church, Garland, Texas, in 1961. He received his B.A. in History, with Honors, from the University of Texas at Austin; his Juris Doctor from University of Houston Law Center—he is a former criminal defense attorney; his Master of Divinity degree from the School of Theology of the University of the South at Sewanee, Tennessee; and his Doctor of Ministry degree from Fuller Theological Seminary in Fullerton, California. He married Varita Gail Michell in 1978; the couple has four children.

He served churches in West Texas (Carrizo Springs, Cotulla, Fredericksburg, and New Braunfels) and West Tennessee (Germantown) before coming to the Diocese of Dallas in 2001 to help the diocese implement its Strategic Plan.

Michell is known throughout the Episcopal Church for his work in congregational development as well as in the governance of the larger church, having led conferences and workshops in over thirty domestic dioceses as well as in Canada. He has served as a deputy to the General Convention four times, serving on several committees, and also has served on the House of Deputies State of the Church Committee as well as serving as its chair. He has also served as a delegate to the Province 7 Synod. The author of two books on congregational development that are used throughout the Episcopal Church and in several of our seminaries, he has also written numerous articles. Additionally, he has served on numerous short-term mission trips: in Mexico; Honduras; Kiev, Ukraine; and South Africa.

He served as the Acting Dean of the Cathedral in 2006 and returned as Acting Dean in 2012-13 and was called as Dean in 2013.

What will be the highlights of his leadership at St. Matthew's Cathedral in the 21st century? Stay tuned and turn to the next chapter.

Dean Michell
Photo credit: Kimberly Durnan
**THE VERY REVEREND NEAL OTIS MICHELL
19**TH **DEAN OF SAINT MATTHEW'S CATHEDRAL**

LOOKING FORWARD

By The Very Reverend Dr. Neal O. Michell
Nineteenth Dean of Saint Matthew's Cathedral

What an exciting time!
    The history of Saint Matthew's Cathedral is full of exciting times. Some generations, I think, experience more excitement than others. Some deans stand out because their times were tempestuous and they rose to the occasion, responding faithfully and leading God's people to achieve important things. Some, quite frankly, did not meet the challenges of their times. Others simply coasted along. It is clear, though, that the present times are among the most challenging.
    How will we respond to the problems of our own generation? The jury is still out. Early indicators are that we are meeting them head-on. Which direction will we choose? Only time will tell.

The Demographic Shift

As I write this chapter, the neighborhood surrounding the cathedral is going through another significant demographic shift. Some of its immigrant families have moved on to other parts of town. They are being partially replaced by other immigrants, mostly from Mexico and African countries, but nevertheless two near-by elementary schools have been closed due to lack of students.

Instead of family houses, the apartment culture of twenty- and-thirty-year-olds is appearing. More and more people - Boomers, Gen X, and Millennials - are putting down roots in the Downtown area and the neighborhoods on its southern perimeter. Lower Greenville Avenue, Henderson Avenue, and Ross Avenue are being revitalized. The City of Dallas, along with other U.S. cities, is experiencing urban renewal, full of young adults rather than family groups.

St. Matthew's has responded to these changes in five important ways.

1. Outreach into the Neighborhood

We have continued and revitalized our Aberg Center for Literacy, Bishop's Camp Summer Reading Program, the Country Fair resale shop, our Food Pantry, and Mi Escuelita Headstart Preschool Program.

We have developed a great partnership with Woodrow Wilson High School, providing hospitality at the Cathedral for several of their events, including evening concerts called "Sunset at the Cathedral," coordinated by Father Stephen Setzer, our 28-year-old curate.

"Summer in the City" teams and volunteer parishioners have held a six-week Summer Vacation Bible School in a vacant lot, attracting 140 children and adults. Several of the families we met on the vacant lot have joined our Parenting Classes. Plans are being laid for reading partners and mentors from Saint Matthew's at an area school.

We have widened our horizon through the arts. Michie Akin, our Music Director, has brought new energy and a strong outreach into the greater arts community of Dallas, and is putting St. Matthew's on the map as a place in Dallas where arts are done well and to the glory of God. He brings love and commitment to the classic role of the cathedral as a center of the arts. With the establishment of St. Matthew's Cathedral Arts, Michie has continued the tradition of excellent classic church music and has brought to the cathedral an even greater involvement in the arts through quarterly Evensong Services, numerous concerts, and the new Justus Sundermann Gallery, which displays the work of fine local artists.

II. Reaching the New Generation

American culture is experiencing a multifaceted phenomenon of spirituality among the 20- and 30- year olds, the first years of the generation known as the Millennials. Although they are not monochromatic, many of them identify themselves as "spiritual but not religious." They eschew rigid denominational labels and are looking for transcendence in their spirituality. We plan to provide this for them.

Like other traditional churches, St. Matthew's has in the past felt an erosion of the number of young adults and households with children among our cathedral family. Now, however, with the addition of Millennial-age clergy (Father David Miller and Father Stephen Setzer), and the many talents of Varita Michell, head of Children's Ministries (Varita is my wife, but it wasn't nepotism. She was hired by the Cathedral before I was), we have seen an influx of young adults, young couples, and young children. Our baptismal font has been busy.

III. Improving Our Facilities

Let's face it. The City of Dallas has never been known for its strong commitment to history or the preservation of its historic buildings. (I continue to be amazed that the handsome arena where the Mavericks and Stars once played was torn down before its 20th birthday.) However, we have to remember that a lot of people came to Texas in the first place to escape the sheriff, or a broken marriage, or debtor's prison, or the wrong politics. They aimed to leave the past behind them. It was the future that mattered.

But we don't have to run away anymore. We don't have to nail a sign on our doors proclaiming GONE TO TEXAS. We're here already. We can honor our past as it deserves.

God has given this congregation a building that is beautiful, timeless in design, and a historical treasure. The walls are soaked with the prayers of God's people for over 100 years. It is our religious as well as civic duty to pass it on to future generations intact. But as our neighborhood has changed, our congregational attendance, membership, and giving have declined, and it has become increasingly difficult to finance needed repairs.

Still, we haven't been idle. My predecessor, Dean Kevin Martin, led the congregation through a capital campaign to refurbish Garrett Hall, our office wing. We have given our beloved cathedral a much-needed face lift; new flooring in the undercroft (basement); the repainting of exterior porches, windows and doors; a new ADA-compliant wheelchair ramp; a new sound system; improved lighting; and a new fire alarm system for both Cathedral and Great Hall. We have purchased new tables and chairs for the Great Hall while refurbishing its Henderson Avenue side and have updated our nursery.

However, much remains to be done. We are currently in the midst of a new capital campaign. It will include projects such as replacing the heating and air conditioning systems in the Cathedral, Great Hall, and kitchen; refinishing the cathedral floors; and completing the refinishing of the third floor of Garrett Hall.

All house owners will recognize that repairs are an ongoing challenge, especially in the case of old buildings. Loving care of our historic Cathedral will be a permanent need.

IV. Challenges of Our Spanish-language Service

Our 12:30 Sunday Service is dedicated to a spiritually lively and healthy Spanish-language congregational life under Father Tony Muñoz. They have done a great job of raising up Spanish-speaking leaders in the Diocese of Dallas, and have helped form clergy in five of the Spanish-speaking Episcopal parishes in our diocese.

Today we face two challenges in this area. As in the case of the English-speaking congregation, many of the Spanish-speaking congregants have also moved to the suburbs. These need to be reclaimed or replaced from within the still large Spanish-speaking community around us. To reach this goal, we need to locate and recruit Spanish speakers who, although fully conversant in English, want to maintain their Latino culture and heritage.

And of course part and parcel of this is the question of how we can come together as a full congregation of Anglo-Hispanic cultures, being both diverse and unified.

V. Quo Vadis?

We must honor the sacrifices of those who have gone before us to bring and preserve our Faith and construct with so much care the beautiful building in which we worship. It is not enough just to sit back and worship God in this cathedral only for our generation. We should appreciate the value of our heritage, yes, but we must always remember that it is not ours alone but that we have an obligation to the generations to come.

**In the name of God we are charged to love,
and preserve, develop, and share.**

Neal Otis Michell+
A.D. 2015

CHRONOLOGY

1529 - Cabeza de Vaca discovers Texas.
1541 - Coronado explores Texas, New Mexico, Oklahoma, and Kansas.
1542 - Luis Mosceso of the DeSoto Expedition visits the future site of Dallas.
1760 - Friar Calahorro y Saenz names the Trinity River.
1771 - Athenese De Miezieres makes a treaty with Indians for territory containing present day Dallas.
1819 - Great American depression.
1820 - Episcopal Church organizes Domestic and Foreign Society.
1821 - First Mexican Republic.
1822 - Mexico becomes an Empire.
1823 - Second Mexican Republic.
1831 - John Wurts Cloud becomes first Episcopal priest to settle in Texas.
1836 - Republic of Texas declared.
1836 - Richard Salmon arrives with five families to establish a Episcopal colony in Texas.
1838 -. Leonidas Polk appointed Missionary Bishop of the Southwest. Caleb Smith Ives appointed first missionary to Republic of Texas.
1841 - Peter's Colony and Mercer's Colony. John Neely Bryant camps on present site of Dallas.
1844 - George Washington Freeman becomes Provisional Bishop of Texas

1846 - Texas joins USA as 28th state.
1849 - First newspaper and first piano arrive in Dallas.
1850 - General Convention admits Texas as new diocese.
1856 - George Rottenstein organizes St. Matthew's Parish.
1859 - Alexander Gregg becomes First Bishop of Texas.
1860 - Great Dallas fire.
1861 - Civil War begins.
1865 - Civil War ends.
1868 - Death of George Rottenstein
1868 - Silas Dean Davenport becomes Rector.
1869 - The arrival of Great Matthew
1870 - First Church (later First Cathedral) Built at Elm and Lamar
1874 - Alexander Charles Garrett becomes 1st Missionary Bishop of Northwest Texas
1875 - 1877 - First Dean - Silas Dean Davenport
1875 - Second Cathedral Built at Commerce and Kendall.
1877 - 1882 - Second Dean - Stephen Hubert Green
1882 - 1884 - Third Dean - John Davis
1884 - 1888 - Fourth Dean - William Mumford
1889 - St. Mary's College founded by Bishop Garrett.
1889 - 1891 - Fifth Dean - Charles William Turner.
1893 - Third Cathedral Built at Canton and Ervay
1894 - 1904 - Sixth Dean - Hudson Stuck
1895 - Alexander Charles Garrett becomes Bishop of Dallas (served until 1924)
1906 - 1917 - Eighth Dean - Harry Tunis Moore
1908 - Dedication of St. Mary's Chapel. (Later Fourth Cathedral)
1918 - 1923 - Ninth Dean - Jackson H. R. Ray
1924 - 1929 - Tenth Dean - Robert Scott Chalmers
1924 - Harry Tunis Moore becomes 2nd Bishop of Dallas
1927 - Ownership of St. Mary's College passes to St. Matthew's.
1929 - We move into our Fourth Cathedral - Ross and Garrett.
1930 - St. Mary's College closes.
1932 - 1940 - Eleventh Dean - George Rodgers Wood

1941 - 1959 - Twelfth Dean - Gerald Grattan Moore
1945 - Charles Avery Mason becomes 3rd Bishop of Dallas.
1959 - 1964 - Thirteenth Dean - Frank Locke Carruthers
1964 - 1987 - Fourteenth Dean - Charles Preston Wiles
1970 - A. Donald Davies becomes 4th Bishop of Dallas
1983 - Donis D. Patterson becomes 5th Bishop of Dallas
1988 - 1992 - Fifteenth Dean - Ernest Edward Hunt III
1992 - 2001 - Sixteenth Dean - Philip M. Duncan II
1993 - James Stanton becomes 6th Bishop of Dallas
2002 - 2005 - Seventeenth Dean - Michael S. Mills
2005 - 2012 - Eighteenth Dean - Kevin E. Martin
2013 - present - Nineteenth Dean – Neal O. Michell

WORKS CONSULTED

Abshire, Richard, *Garland, A Contemporary History*, Historical Publishing Network, San Antonio, 2009.

Beasley, Claude A., *The Episcopal Church in Northern Texas Until 1890*, Wichita Falls, Texas, 1952

Brown, John Henry, *History of Dallas County, Texas, from 1837-1887*. Aldredge Book Store, Dallas, 1966.

Brown, Lawrence L., *The Episcopal Church in Texas, 1838-1871*, Church Historical Society, Austin, 1963.

Cabeza de Vaca, Alvar Numez, *Adventures in the Unknown Interior of America*, translated by Cycone Covey, University of New Mexico, Albuquerque, 1961.

Cochran, John H., *Dallas County: A Record of Its Pioneers and Progress*. Aldredge Book Store, Dallas, 1966.

Dallas Morning News

Dallas Times Herald

Dealey, Ted, *Diaper Days of Dallas*, Abingdon Press, NY, 1966.

Dean, David M., *Breaking Trail: Hudson Stuck of Texas and Alaska*, Ohio University Press, Athens, 1988.

Fehrenbach, T. R., *Lone Star*, American Legacy Press, New York, 1983.

Giles, Marie, *Early History of Medicine in Dallas 1841-1900*. UT Thesis. 1950.

Harvey, Robert C., *To the Isles Afar Off*, Four Directions Press, Rhinebeck, New York, 2009.

Hazel, Michael V., *Dallas, A History of Big D*, Texas State Historical Association, Austin, 1997.

Howard, John Tasker, *Stephen Foster: America's Troubadour*, Thomas Y. Crowell Company, New York, 1934.

Howard, Louise M., *The History of Saint Matthew's Cathedral*, Dallas, Texas, 1923.

Hunt III, Ernest Edward, *Sermon Struggles*, The Seabury Press, 1982

Hutchinson, Mary Foster, *Texian Odyssey*, Sunbelt Eaken Press, Austin, 2003.

Hutchinson, Mary Foster, *How the Faith Came to Dallas*, Dallas, 2011.

Jones, C. Allen, *Texas Roots*, Texas A&M University Press, College Station 2001.

MacDonald, William L. III, *Dallas Rediscoered*, Dallas Historical Society, 1978.

Moore, Gerald G., *The Diocese of Dallas 1895-1952*, Dallas, Texas, 1952.

Muir, Andrew Forest, (Editor), *Texas in 1837*, University of Texas Press, Austin, 1986.

Murchison, William, *Mortal Follies*, Encounter Books, New York, 2009

Nevin, David, *The Texans - What They Are and Why*, William Morrow and Company, New York 1968

Newcombe, W. W., Jr., *The Indians of Texas*, University of Texas Press, 1961.

New Handbook of Texas in Six Volumes, Texas State Historical Association, Austin, 1996.

Pioneer Families of Dallas County, Proud Heritage Two, Dallas County Pioneer Association, 1993.

Prichard, Robert, *A History of the Episcopal Church*, Morehouse Publishing, Harrisburg, Penn., 1999.

Ray, Dr. J. H. Randolph, *My Little Church Around the Corner*, Simon and Schuster, New York, 1957.

Roberts, Larenda Lyles, and Theadgill, Kay, *Dallas Uncovered*, Seaside Press, Plano, 1998.

Rogers, John William, *The Lusty Texans of Dallas*, Dutton and Company, New York, 1951.

Rumbley, Rose-Mary, *The Unauthorized History af Dallas, Texas*, Eakin Press, Austin, 1991.

Samuels, Nancy T., and Knox, Barbara, *Old Northwest Texas, Navarro County, 1846-1860*, Fort Worth Genealogical Society, 1980.

Stuck, Hudson, *The Ascent of Denali,* (Mount McKinley), Charles Scribners Sons. New York, 1914.

Texas Declaration of Independence, Highlands Historical Press Inc., Dallas, 1953.

The Right Reverend Alexander Charles Garrett, A. C. Garrett Council No. 382, Royal and Select Masters, R. W. Cooper, Thrice Illustrious Master, 1980.

Thetford and Tabb, Editors, *Bishop Garrett's Journals 1875-1890*, Dallas, Texas, 1981.

Thompson, Oscar, (Editor), *Cyclopedia of Music and Musicians*, Dodd Mead and Company, New York 1952.

Wikipedia, the Free Enyclopedia.

Wiles, C. Preston, *Windows of Faith*, Dallas, 2001.

Wiles, C. Preston, *The Episcopal Diocese of Dallas, a Centennial Narrative History*, Dallas, 1995.

Worthen, Mary Fletcher, *The History of Trinity, The Cathedral of the Episcopal Diocese of Arkansas, 1884-1995*, August House Publishers, Inc., Little Rock, 1996.

WPA Guide and History, Dallas Public Library, Texas Center for the Book, University of North Texas Press, 1992.

Wright, Nicolas Thomas, *Surprised By Hope*, Harper One, NY, 2008.

Wylie, Sam and Andrew, *Texas Got It Right*, Dallas, 2012.

ACKNOWLEDGEMENTS

Writing history is rather like working a very large jigsaw puzzle. Here are some of the kind-hearted people who found missing pieces for me, fit some very odd shapes together, and helped me to make sense of time, place, and perspective: Thank you, generous people. I could have done it without you, but not without leaving lots of empty holes.

MFH

H. Michie Akin
The Rt. Rev. William Anderson, Bishop of Caledonia
Bryan Cather, St. John's Church, St. Louis
Phyllis Creighton Danby
Mark Doty, City of Dallas Heritage Commission
David Farrell
Holly Farrell
Whittier Hamers
Harvard University Botany Department
Dr. M. Hollis Hutchinson
William Henry Hutchinson
Robert Jones
Wayne Kempton, Archivist, Cathedral of St. John the Divine, NYC
The Rev. Travis C. Koerner, Christ Church Cathedral, New Orleans
The Rev. Canon George E. Luck
The Very Rev. Kevin Martin
The Rev. Paul K. McLain III, Trinity Cathedral, Little Rock

The Rt. Rev. Dr. Logan McMenamie, Bishop of British Columbia
Michael McNeely
William Murchison
The Rev. David Miller
The Rev. Canon Antonio Munoz
Anne Petrimonox, Archivist, Trinity Church, NYC
Susan G. Rehkopf, Archivist, Diocese of Saint Louis
Mary Robison, Reference Librarian, General Seminary, NYC
Seventh Floor of the Dallas Public Library
Pat Shaughnessy
The Rev. H. Edward Sholty
Dr. Alan Skinner
Jim Stillson
Barbara Turner, Archivist of the Diocese of Dallas
Mary Worthen
Dr. Peter Yasenchak, Schuylkill, Historical Society

Printed in the United States
By Bookmasters